Jennifer Bilek is one of the most brilliant and courageous people I've ever met. Like a prophet, she shakes us out of our slumber to confront the 'trans' assault on our humanity. It is, as her blog is called, *The 11th Hour*. For yourselves, your loved ones, and for our civilization, put down what you are doing, read this book, and join this epic battle.
　—Miriam Grossman, MD, psychiatrist and author of
　　Lost in Trans Nation: A Child Psychiatrist's Guide Out
　　of the Madness

Jennifer Bilek remains a unique and heroic figure in revealing the truth of transhumanism and its impact on women and children. She scrupulously follows the money and concepts that are the foundations of the transhumanist industrial complex and alerts us to the social transformations waiting for us down the line. Everyone concerned about protecting the integrity of women's and children's bodies from theft by men – already eroded by gender identity ideology – should read this book so that we can be armed for the future.
　—Heather Brunskell-Evans, author of *Transgender Body Politics*

Transsexual Transgender Transhuman is sharply investigated and clearly written for anyone approaching the social contagion that has united many on the left and the right against the industrial gender industry that has taken hold of anglophone societies for the past fifteen years. Jennifer Bilek's book peels off, layer by layer, the financial backers of the gender industry and its roots within academia, Big Pharma, Big Tech, and the managerial professional class that traffics in utter anti-scientific hokum.
　—Julian Vigo, Anthropologist, journalist, writer, editor
　　of *Savage Minds*

You must read Jennifer Bilek's book to gird yourself against the onslaught of the technocratic cult of transhumanism that's attacking our children, our personal relationships, and our very humanity. Jennifer Bilek is a brilliant prophet who connects the dots with clarity, precision, and prescience.

—Stella Morabito, author of *The Weaponization of Loneliness* and senior contributor at *The Federalist*

Jennifer Bilek has been at the forefront for years, reporting on the massive wealth pushing today's 'transgender' propaganda. Her work has helped countless others fighting against the delusion that it is possible to change one's sex. She names names, the organizations, and the foundations funding this movement to the tune of billions. If you need one book on your shelf that provides answers, this book is it.

—Jennifer Lahl, Founder, The Center for Bioethics and Culture, author, and filmmaker

Photo credit: Chris Casler

Jennifer Bilek is an investigative journalist who has tracked the funding of the gender industry for over a decade. She is author of *The 11th Hour*, a platform highlighting the connections between technology, transsexualism, and transhumanism. Her research into the philanthropic backers of the gender industry has been utilized for legal briefs, and platformed in myriad publications, films, and other media in the US and internationally. She has appeared on *The Megyn Kelly Show*, Steven Bannon's *War Room,* and James Patrick's *Big Picture*, and on various feminist platforms and podcasts. She has been featured in films such as *No Way Back* (2023), *Gender Transformation* (2023), and *The Gender Delusion* (2023). Her work has been published in numerous books and magazines, among which: *First Things, Tablet, Human Events, The Federalist, The American Mind*, and in the feminist anthology, *Female Erasure*.

TRANSSEXUAL TRANSGENDER TRANSHUMAN

Dispatches from the 11th Hour

Jennifer Bilek

We respectfully acknowledge the wisdom of Aboriginal and Torres Strait Islander peoples and their custodianship of the lands and waterways. The Countries on which Spinifex offices are situated are Djiru, Bunurong and Wurundjeri, Wadawurrung, Gundungarra and Noongar.

First published by Spinifex Press, 2024

Spinifex Press Pty Ltd
PO Box 200, Little River, VIC 3211, Australia
PO Box 105, Mission Beach, QLD 4852, Australia
women@spinifexpress.com.au
www.spinifexpress.com.au

Edited by Renate Klein, Susan Hawthorne and Pauline Hopkins
Cover design by Deb Snibson
All photos reproduced in this book are sourced from Creative Commons unless otherwise specified.
Typesetting by Helen Christie, Blue Wren Books
Typeset in Minion
Printed in the USA

ISBN: 9781922964106 (paperback)
ISBN: 9781922964113 (ebook)

For my parents

Links have been provided for the original online publication in the footnote on the first page of each article. All online sources include links for any reader wanting to follow up the references.

Contents

Introduction

Censorship is advertising paid by the government.

—Frederico Fellini

In my research and writing I follow the money behind the gender industry, a domineering and monied business pursuit with a very powerful lobby which is advanced as a human rights campaign. The gender industry is the promotion of the adult male fetish of transsexualism, rebranded for today's youth, grooming them for industrial body dissociation.

Behind the slogans about freedom of expression, and euphemisms such as 'gender care' and 'gender dysphoria' is a marketing apparatus so unrelenting and extreme, it has acted upon the populace like cult indoctrination. It has captured large swaths of the public imagination, corporations, educational and medical institutions, and governments across the western world and beyond, by the idea that the human sex boundary between males and females is a social construct.

As early as 2002, the letter 'T' was added to the LGB acronym. LGB NGOs in the state of California tacked it on with little awareness by mainstream culture of what it would come to mean. By 2007, it gained traction and more LGB NGOs added the T. Purportedly, a new marginalized and special sexual orientation needed protection. This added entity was poised to upend our societies, languages, and laws, organized around our species' reproductive sex, the fact that we are males and females. A few years later, the idea that human reproductive sex exists on a spectrum began to take hold in English-speaking societies, defying billions of years of biological evolution,

1

and hundreds of thousands of years of human evolution. Biological reproduction in humans, reportedly, was discovered to have been a mistake. The new identities, emerging with T, needed the medical industrial complex (MIC) to assist people in finding their true natures.

Living in America, home of Big Pharma, I smelled money.

My journey down the rabbit hole of the vast funding and political apparatus of the now LGBTIQ+ began in 2013, when it dawned on me something was terribly wrong with what people were calling 'the left'.

This dawning happened gradually. I voted for Obama in his first run for president, suffering a bad case of 'hope-nosis' like many on the political left, hoping beyond hope perhaps, that our society's slip into the long, dark, night of authoritarianism and ruling corporate greed could be stopped.

Inheriting the financial meltdown in America after his inauguration in 2009, President Obama bailed out the big banks to the tune of $800 billion. It was the biggest banking bailout ever, with complete impunity for the fraudsters at the center of the averted meltdown. The Pritzkers, a billionaire American family at the heart of the burgeoning gender industry scam, had a heavy hand in the crisis of excessive mortgage lending to borrowers who normally would not qualify for a home loan. But I didn't know about the Pritzkers, or their relationship to Obama, until much later. I only knew that complete impunity for those who caused the problem didn't seem like any kind of justice from a newly elected democratic president, one whose campaign rested on restoring hope for Americans.

By September 2011, my activist heart was lured down to the financial district of New York City, which isn't far from my home. It was ground zero for Occupy Wall Street (OWS), a 59-day, left-wing populist movement against economic inequality and the influence of money in politics. The movement began in Zuccotti Park, located near Wall Street, an eight-block-long row of streets in the Financial District.

Culminative frustration about the financial and social influence of big banks and Wall Street spearheaded the uprising that turned into an encampment. The response to the bailout of elites and their golden parachutes sparked the flame. The height of the movement in Zuccotti Park lasted until 15 November 2011. It sputtered on for a bit longer, after the occupation, but with the camps and the visibility of a people's political uprising gone, it was virtually dead.

Stepping out of the subway system on a cool September morning in 2011, the energy of OWS, a potentially volcanic uprising, was galvanizing. I could feel the current on my skin. I didn't know it then, but that crackling energy in Zuccotti Park was to become a funeral pyre, the place the political left, as I had known it, came to die. Workers' unions, civil rights for blacks, women, and the same-sex attracted, along with anti-war and environmental protests, were all laid to rest there. The acceleration of Environmental, Social, and Corporate Governance (ESG) and Diversity, Equity, and Inclusion (DEI) policies, devised in the 1980s, were the specters that rose rapidly out of the ashes of the political left, along with gender identity ideology. These policies have grown out of the 1960s movement for divestment from Apartheid in South Africa before it came to the fore in the mid-1980s, when corporations began to divest, or invest, their capital toward social change.

Obama went on to become our first 'trans' president, passing human rights laws for those who attempted to disown their sexed reality, who were emerging on the social and political landscape in droves and taking the helm of key political positions. Amanda Simpson, a man appropriating womanhood, became Obama's first 'transgender' presidential appointee. He was appointed to the position of Senior Technical Adviser in the Bureau of Industry and Security at the US Department of Commerce.

It took until 2020 for the ESG and DEI policies to have a real stranglehold on many western cultures. Since 2020, there have been advancing incentives from the United Nations (UN) to systematize ESG policies, corporately, culturally, institutionally, and globally. This framework, used to assess an organization's business practices and performance, based on various sustainability and ethical issues, are joint initiatives of financial institutions at the invitation of the UN. In less than 20 years, the ESG/DEI movement has grown from a corporate social responsibility initiative launched by the UN into a global phenomenon representing more than $30 trillion in assets under management. It basically hands over social and political responsibility to oligarchs, corporatists, and financial assets management firms like Ernst & Young and BlackRock, which invest in the future equality and sustainability goals of what they hope will become a global society, with homogenized virtues, ethics, goals, and initiatives. This process usurps the power of people to create culture and society through governance and the election of officials that speak and act for the citizens of the world's many diverse populations. Social justice movements, versus real political resistance to corporate hegemony and human rights violations, have become the mouthpiece of these corporatists and oligarchs who are funding their version of equality, not that of the people.

These ESG and DEI policies have morphed into a global agenda known as the UN Agenda 2030 for Sustainable Development Goals (SDG). Around 2014, the time the term 'transgender' entered the American cultural landscape in full force, "a coalition of concerned human rights organizations working to counter the exclusion of persons due to real or perceived sexual orientation, gender identity, gender expression, and bodily diversity" petitioned for a seat at the SDG UN agenda table, with their SDG Zero Draft Outcome Document. 'Bodily diversity' is the key component of all the current discussions of gender bills, laws, and expression. The bodily diversity being promoted in laws across western societies, in the name of gender, manifests the illusion of another type of person, beyond the borders of our reproductive sex, and thereby our humanity.

Under the new ESG system, corporatists and oligarchs buy a seat at the UN table for assessing global governance and DEI goals, to provide all the justice and equality we need. For those of us unwilling to go along with hegemony posing as diversity, Orwell-style, the hammer of financial threat, censorship, and bullying is coming down upon us, whether we are an individual, an institution, a business or a corporation. It is tyranny, American style. This is how the strong political uprisings of the former left, that impacted society in beneficial ways, were usurped by corporate and philanthropic funding and became unhinged ideologies stumping for the corporate state, while those of us on the former political left are still standing agog at the wreckage.

The funerary rites in Zuccotti Park lasted 59 days, though participants didn't know it was the end of all the left stood for. At its core, the left was a movement that cared about the people and the environment over corporations. Erin Brockovich and Karen Silkwood would have fit right in at Zuccotti Park in 2011.

Before the occupation descended into homeless encampments and was infiltrated by state operatives, the OWS resistance emerged as an organic rebellion kicked off by a couple of Canadians. Two young people who worked for a Canadian anti-consumerist collective, Adbusters, set up a website announcing a directive toward other young people, saddled with enormous college tuitions. People were called on to set up tents inside the park. The tents created a colorful mosaic. People carried posters and played music. Various companies like Ben & Jerry's brought in ice cream and food for the squatters. They were there to shine a spotlight on the corporate conglomerates and the banks (those recently bailed out to avert a gargantuan financial collapse), overtaking American society. Their slogan was 'We Are the 99%'.

Though the movement was started by those on the left, it soon became a movement of the people against the 1%, the uber-rich, without the strict left/right divide. It seemed to be assembling into a real class struggle for a change, which was part of its electricity, its power.

The faults of OWS were many, unfortunately, but its genius was the encampments, where people gathered to talk to each other, off-line, and send messages to the public, that were not allowed by

5

state-backed media conglomerates. It was the daily, impassioned, conversations of the people there that proved threatening to the state, and which fueled the development of the movement.

Activist engineers offered their services to report on the developments inside the park. Tents were set aside for the computers, speakers, and film crews. The movement grew swiftly. By 9 October 2011, Occupy protests had taken place or were ongoing in over 951 cities across 82 countries, and in over 600 communities in the United States. People from all walks of life turned up during the day to talk to each other about what was happening to the 99% of American citizens, while the uber-rich were rolling like swine in mud, gorging on stock, mortgage, and money laundering fraud, perfectly illustrated by Leonardo DiCaprio's character in *The Wolf of Wall Street* film. Families and couples, activists and housewives of every color and religious stripe, were congregating. It felt like a neighborhood party with an urgent purpose. Having a foot that was newly healed from being broken, I walked over the Brooklyn Bridge, with a cane in one hand, in a protest that was at least 40,000 people strong.

Gender ideology was not on our cultural radar yet, but conversations about the reality of wealth transfer from the middle class to the already rich proved as dangerous for the elite oligarchs of Wall Street as any critique of gender ideology has become today for corporate power.

The dismantling of tents, and the potential for change, was just as swift as its emergence. All those passionate speeches by left-wing icons, Naomi Klein, Cornel West, and Chris Hedges among them, the posters confronting the 1%, the oil and banking tycoons, and the other oligarchs ruining American lives, the marches, the excitement, and the independent media recording it all, faded quickly. At the end of November 2011, in the middle of the night, searchlights, helicopters, and police with loud sirens and batons descended on the various parks with OWS activists, ripping people from their tents and tearing up their makeshift homes for the past two months. Panic and havoc ensued. It was a terrible foretelling of things to come for the left, which in the years to follow seemed to abandon all its principles and start stumping for the very corporatism they were initially resisting.

I grew my sea legs as an investigative journalist during OWS, writing articles for a friend's photojournalism chronicling the events there. As I continued campaigning for women's rights, something I had done since I was in my twenties, and fighting for the health of the environment, something terrible was happening. I could feel it.

In the years following the near meltdown of the market, and the dismantling of OWS, the strong stench of a quickly growing authoritarianism began to emerge in activist circles. The burgeoning authoritarianism which grew to the extreme in the aftermath of the 9/11 attacks had not yet reached the peak of the Edward Snowden and WikiLeaks exposures. But it was turning in the wrong direction, and you could feel the totalitarianism settling in.

Being a painter my entire life, I am trained to see what others can't or won't see and to give the unseen, the unsaid, a vision or a voice. I excel at the bird's eye view, as well as being able to examine the minutiae of any given situation. With the gift of sight, there comes an intense impulse to speak, to show, and to help others understand what is being observed. Artists can be seen as intense and dramatic for this reason. What I saw developing all around me was a renewed McCarthyism. This budding McCarthyism took hold fast and spread rapaciously, including through universities. Speech was being shut down and people were framed as traitors and bigots. The practice of publicizing accusations of disloyalty to minority populations especially, on social media and beyond, was running rampant. In 2013, I took up researching the money going to the LGBT NGO political apparatus, because a particularly virulent strain of this new McCarthyism seemed to be inhabiting it. Activist friends were having their platforms canceled, with no place left to speak. People invested in the promotion of gender ideology were especially vocal about the added 'T', and protecting it, though no one seemed very clear on what that was, or why a small group of men with a fetish for dressing up as women needed the protection of world governments, corporations, legal bodies, and university heads. University students would show up at various conferences to oppose any mention of biological reality. In environmental activism, mentioning biological reality was hard to avoid. The same was true for women's rights, as women all over the world are oppressed because of our biology.

By June 2013, Penny Pritzker, of the billionaire Chicagoan Pritzkers, was appointed Obama's Secretary of Commerce, and her cousin James (now Jennifer) released a statement to his employees at Tawani Enterprises and the Pritzker Military Library indicating that he was now a woman. Pritzker would be the world's first 'transgender' billionaire. It was the same year Edward Snowden, a computer intelligence consultant and whistleblower, leaked highly classified information from the National Security Agency about global surveillance. This disclosure is important to the story of the emergence of gender ideology in the American landscape because along with its emergence came an even more accentuated lack of sexual privacy. Fetishes, kink, and bondage were all let out of the proverbial closet and into family parades, children's story hours, their classroom curricula, and the corporate board rooms of major banks.

Tawani Enterprises is an entrepreneurial organization that functions to preserve historic landmarks and neighborhood development, and a venture capital firm which partners with Squadron Capital, another private equity firm investing in predominantly medical and technology corporations. It is also a philanthropic organization, providing capital that drives gender ideology. Pritzker's announcement to his staff read:

> As of August 16, 2013, J. N. Pritzker will undergo an official legal name change, will now be known as Jennifer Natalya Pritzker. This change will reflect the beliefs of her true identity that she has held privately and will now share publicly. Pritzker now identifies herself as a woman for all business and personal undertakings.

Poof! Like a genie from a bottle, this happened as if by magic, and there was a lot more of it to come.

In 2014, a male actor going by the name of Laverne Cox, and posing as a woman, ushered in what was called a 'transgender tipping point' on the cover of *Time* magazine in America. The following year, American sports icon, Bruce Jenner, then going by Caitlyn, announced he had always been a woman. To much fanfare and accolades from the media and the public, he posed on the cover of *Vanity Fair*, a national fashion magazine, in a woman's corset. Simultaneously, a Melbourne-raised male model was taking center stage at *Vogue* in Paris. Andreja Pejic, also an activist, rose to fame after staking his claim to womanhood. In the years since, he's fronted a torrent of campaigns, editorials, and runway shows for Marc Jacobs, *Vogue*, Jean Paul Gaultier, H&M, DKNY and Jeremy Scott, and he recently re-signed a lucrative contract as the face of Makeup For Ever.

Suddenly, the idea of mystically, alternately sexed humans, was everywhere. Children were born in the wrong bodies, and people were suffering horrible body dysphoria and were considered brave and amazing if they had their reproductive organs medically assaulted to appear as the opposite sex.

As a campaigner for women's rights, I was well versed on the adult male fetish of transsexualism, and the men who engaged in it, because of their early historical attempts to transgress women's boundaries, especially lesbians', and women's resistance to their efforts, but this seemed to be getting a rebranding. It was suddenly being marketed as 'progressive', just another way to be human, and the target market was children and young people.

Then came non-binary identities, nullos, and asexual people, all clamoring for a piece of the oppression pie, and screaming down anyone who asked questions about these identities. It was pronounced repeatedly that attempting to disown one's sexed reality was a human right. Following quickly on the heels of these strange pronouncements were the avowals that these were not just subjective identities, but that reproductive sex existed on a spectrum and men who claimed to be women *were* women. Year in and year out, the ante kept getting raised. Laws were changed to accommodate attempts at disowning one's sexed reality, all being framed and forced onto society as a human right.

What ESG policies do for the broader culture, namely homogenize it while dictating social behavior, through organizations like Businesses for Social Responsibility (BSR), Principles for Responsible Investing (PRI), the Human Rights Campaign (HRC), and PGLE, or Partnership for Global LGBT Equality, do for the new body-denying concept of gender ideology. As they intersect with the global LGBT NGOs and political apparatus, they force people and organizations to adopt gender ideology. PRI and BSR are part of the UN human rights corporate investment strategy. PGLE is a coalition of 29 organizations purportedly committed to leveraging their individual and collective advocacy to accelerate LGBT equality and inclusion in the workplace globally, and in the communities in which they operate.

HRC is a conglomerate of forces that are working to instill gender ideology throughout American culture. Their corporate equality index, which offers credit scores for behavior that supports the $4.7 trillion marketing constituency that is LGBT, is very successful (updated April 2024, <https://www.lgbt-capital. com/index.php?menu_id=2>). Corporations, law firms, schools, prisons, sports organizations, religious and medical institutions, all embrace the LGBT message. They understand that if they don't, they will be locked out of the market. In concert, these ESG entities work like a cartel, to instill an ideology of disowning sexed reality as progressive, via the LGBT human rights political infrastructure, into the market, corporate culture, institutions, and our communities.

By 2016, Jordan Peterson, a professor and a practitioner of psychiatry in Canada, was being publicly castigated for not agreeing to any legal mandate that would have him calling a man a woman, or using a female pronoun for him. He rose to become a formidable public persona and commentator because of his continuing stand against this budding state tyranny. A graduate student and teaching assistant at Wilfrid Laurier University (WLU) in Waterloo, Ontario, Lyndsay Shepard was subjected to an inquisition by the university, simply for playing one of Peterson's speeches in her class and asking questions. WLU is partnered with a think tank in Waterloo, funded by George Soros, another major player in the gender industry.

2017 also gave birth to the Yogyakarta Principles (YP) plus 10. A decade after the initial YP principles of 2007 were established as a statement of the human rights for people with LGB sexual orientations, the plus 10 was created. The YP plus 10 document is an attempt to bring gender identity ideology, a completely amorphous and materially unsound concept, into international human rights law. It constructs fictitious violations suffered by people who purportedly have what is called a "gender identity at odds with their sex characteristics." The social and legal priority is given to the materially unsound concept of their gender feelings as referenced in the YP plus 10. In short, it is an attempt to legally tie a concept of dissociation from sexed reality to our human rights apparatus through our human rights entities. Though the YPs are not law, they are often treated as such.

Around this same time, I had also begun to publish some of my findings regarding the commodification of human reproductive sex, which I saw happening under the LGBT banner of human rights. I wrote a piece with a colleague and fellow campaigner for women's rights, Mary Ceallaigh, for *Female Erasure: What You Need to Know about Gender Politics' War on Women, the Female Sex and Human Rights* (2016). Our article, 'In The Absence of the Sacred: The Marketing of Medical Transgenderism and the Survival of the Natural Child', addressed the issue of medicalizing children's subjective identities for profit, in conjunction with a technological assault on children, via cell phones, social media, video games and pornography. Our thesis focused on Jazz Jennings, now a man who claims womanhood for himself, who began being exploited by his family and the media, and promoted as a 'transgender child' when he was just two years old. Jazz liked sparkles and mermaids and soon became the poster child for promoting dissociation from sexed reality as a progressive new lifestyle for young people. He catapulted the launch of the adult male fetish of transsexualism into a medical-tech industry identity for young people. His reality TV show, *I Am Jazz*, begun in 2015, serialized the horror of having his healthy reproductive system medically assaulted, several times, for entertainment. *People* magazine documented his pre-castration celebration, complete with a penis goodbye cake.

This was the moment of my descent into the matrix of financial backing for an industry selling dissociation from sexed reality as progressive. This industry, and its formation out of the autogynephilic fetish of adult men, reduces women to commoditized parts to assuage their fixations. It doesn't matter if all transsexuals are fetishists. Some men with internalized homophobia have taken a similar path in attempting to disown their sex, and now many young women with internalized homophobia are doing the same. But the fetish is what is being marketed as progressive: dissociation from the sexed body, male ownership of womanhood reduced to parts, and women as objects of sexual fixation, have flourished with new technological and pharmacological advancements. Two generations of the sexual objectification of women in pornography brought into every household, and now normalized in the music industry and elsewhere, has given it wings.

Society, laws, and language are being rapidly overhauled because of this compulsion. Human beings, especially women, are far more profitable as parts than we are as wholly sexed beings. This is the fetishization of human sex cut up for the market. It has been rebranded as 'transgenderism' to groom youth into body dissociation, opening them up for commercialization and experimentation for the engineering of our species.

This is a transhumanist paradigm that has legally constructed the transsexual/'transgender' child to support the normalization of this fetish. By 2016, I knew this was what was happening, but I wanted to know why and how it was happening. I wanted to share my research and organize a seminar, to be held at the Left Forum (LF) in New York City. "If you want to learn, teach," is an old and appropriate adage here. I wanted to learn what others thought of what I was finding. The LF is an annual political conference, boasting the largest gathering of the political left, which lasts for three days. What are now known as 'trans activists' swarmed the venue, with claims that my talk was violent. The venue caved to their tyranny and apologized to them. It did not escape me that the political left, long a bastion of free speech, including the protection of porn under its auspices, was censoring mine. At this point, I understood that I was absolutely on the right path to disclosing a newly minted industry grooming people into intimate violations of their anatomy – and posing it as a human right.

What gender ideology does is position the dissociation from sexed reality as a *right*. It socially skews reproductive sex and the way we organize our societies around it. It seeks protection for those who claim to be outside the borders of human sexual dimorphism as it decimates the rights of women, parents, and homosexuals, and violates the bodies and instincts of children. It promotes a transcendence from our humanness, grounded in sex. The wreckage of once-healthy families across America and elsewhere is growing steadily because of it. Society, laws, language, and institutions, supported by international corporations, law firms, and investment houses, along with governments, are being overhauled to assimilate females into males, to obliterate the sex boundary toward a tech takeover of human reproduction, and eventually, humanity itself.

Today, the new McCarthyism has escalated to the point that in 2023, Kellie-Jay Keen, a women's rights campaigner in the UK, was almost trampled by a large, aggressive mob in New Zealand. She would have been crushed by what are being called 'trans rights activists' if not for her security detail, for organizing a rally to allow women to speak about their humanity. Ms Keen is particularly dangerous for this agenda because she, like the OWS movement before her, has circumvented the corporately controlled mainstream media which is funded by Big Pharma, Big Tech, and Big Finance. She has inspired women, globally, to get into the streets and talk to each other about what is happening. For the audacious claim that women are adult human females, Kellie-Jay Keen has been treated to the most authoritarian stranglehold of censorship of perhaps anyone speaking about this issue today. On 4 November 2023 she stated on social media:

> Sometimes the pinch of censorship is very strong and weighs heavy.
>
> As a reminder, I am banned from: Patreon, Change.org (can't even sign a petition), Mumsnet, Eventbrite, Give butter, Crowdfunder, Gofundme, TikTok, Link tree, LinkedIn Prime Site and other billboard companies. These companies refuse to make things for me: Teespring, Awesome merchandise, Hello print. These companies refuse to allow me to sell merch or advertise on their platforms: Facebook, and Instagram. I have been demonetized from YouTube and throttled (people who subscribe don't get notifications). I have been throttled on X after a four-and-a-half-year ban (most people are prevented from seeing my posts and even people who follow me find it difficult to see anything I post, I can't even be found by searching my name. However, malicious parody accounts can be found by searching my name).
>
> Venues won't host my meetings. Hotels have canceled my booking at short notice.
>
> Even a shop assistant thought they could accuse me of standing with Nazis (I won't go into the police, routine defamation from all sides including global media, minor celebrities, and politicians.) Therefore, I focus on real-life events in the open. I have nothing to hide. I don't put any of my content behind a paywall or ask people to subscribe for extra content. I want everyone to keep hearing the truth and to know that it is possible to speak it, without fear. I want women to know that they have the right to speak about their rights, their lives, and concerns for their loved ones posed by the lie that is transgender bullshit. Women are enough to focus on our needs, without apology. Censorship hurts the message that I'm trying to get out.

Andy Ngo, an American journalist, author, and social media influencer known for covering and video-recording demonstrators, was recently awarded $300,000 in a judgment over Portland Antifa after being beaten by them at a demonstration. Antifa is a big supporter of the medical assault on healthy human reproductive sex and is often violent at protests by women's rights campaigns. Even wealthy public figures such as author J.K. Rowling, the British author of the Harry Potter book series, and Dave Chappelle, an American comedian, have had their day of public whippings in the town square for not going along with an ideology that goes against everything we know about our human nature.

After a decade of research, I assess that gender propaganda is not ultimately about sexed expressions. An endless number of discussions and arguments can be had regarding the word 'gender'. We've been engaged in them since the sexual revolution and with renewed fervor since the conjuring of synthetic sex identities by the techno-medical complex.

This remains a distraction from the industry of body dissociation – transhumanism – that is being cultivated and is still in its infancy. This new paradigm is the reason changes to our language, law, and societies have become so important. I'm convinced the industry normalizing dissociation from sexed reality, the very foundation of what makes us human, needs to be the focus of our resistance going forward. This industry has built a legal human rights apparatus to change our species' borders.

As the journalist, Stella Morabito, has written, "Transgenderism is a vehicle for state power and censorship." It is tyranny dressed up in the clothes of what has become the carcass of the progressive left, and it seeks absolute power and control over humanity and nature.

Resistance to what amounts to a technological religious cult being orchestrated through the very technology those in power want to meld us with, must become a love story for our time. Defiance against our enslavement to a mechanized life, and protection of the children who will inhabit this earth and hopefully their bodies after we're gone, should fuel exhilaration, not despair.

We have but one life and if we use it to help each other, then failure is impossible.

I started publishing my blog, *The 11th Hour*, in 2020, to share my findings, some of which I include in this book. I hope my essays inspire you to resist this anti-human agenda, to stand with courage and in solidarity, to protect the future for all our children, and to protect the boundaries of women.

#1

Who are the rich, white men institutionalizing transgender ideology?[1]

Note to readers

At the time this article, written in 2017, was published, I was still referring to people who attempt to disown their sex through medical technology as 'transgender'. Most people still make this reference. I now understand that 'transgender' is not a type of person, as no one transcends their sex, and that this is no more than a construct being legally, corporately, and institutionally cultivated.

'Transgenderism' is an umbrella term under which sit too many conflicting ideas. As a type of person, it does not make sense, and obscures the legal, social, linguistic, political, and material disasters being manifested in its name. Since the posts in this book span the years 2018-present, some refer to 'transgenderism' and to some people as 'transgender'. Later publications refer to synthetic sex identities, and people who attempt to disown their sex.

* * *

As an environmental activist who was already deplatformed from a speaking venue by transactivists in 2013, I developed curiosity about the power of this group to force such a development. A year later, when *TIME* magazine announced a transgender tipping point on its cover, I had already begun to examine the money behind the transgender project.

I have watched as all-women's safe spaces, universities, and sports opened their doors to any man who chose to identify as a woman. Whereas men who identify as transwomen are at the

---

1   First published 20 February 2018, *The Federalist*. <https://thefederalist.com/2018/02/20/rich-white-men-institutionalizing-transgender-ideology/>

forefront of this project, women who identify as transmen seem silent and invisible. I was astonished that such a huge cultural change as the opening of sex-protected spaces was happening at such a meteoric pace and without consideration for women and girls' safety, deliberation, or public debate.

Concurrent with these rapid changes, I witnessed an overhaul in the English language with new pronouns and a near-tyrannical assault on those who did not use them. Laws mandating new speech were passed. Laws overriding biological sex with the amorphous concept of gender identity are being instituted now. People who speak openly about these changes can find themselves, their families, and their livelihoods threatened.

These elements, along with media saturation of the issue, had me wondering: Is this really a civil rights issue for a tiny part of the population with body dysphoria, or is there a bigger agenda with moneyed interests that we are not seeing? This article can only begin to graze the surface of this question but considering transgenderism has basically exploded in the middle of capitalism, which is notorious for subsuming social justice movements, there is value in beginning this examination.

Who is funding the transgender movement?

I found exceedingly rich, white men with enormous cultural influence are funding the transgender lobby and various transgender organizations. These include but are not limited to Jennifer Pritzker (a male who identifies as transgender); George Soros; Martine Rothblatt (a male who identifies as transgender and transhumanist); Tim Gill (a gay man); Drummond Pike; Warren and Peter Buffett; Jon Stryker (a gay man); Mark Bonham (a gay man); and Ric Weiland (a deceased gay man whose philanthropy is still LGBT-oriented). Most of these billionaires fund the transgender lobby and organizations through their own organizations, including corporations.

President Joe Biden talks with Illinois Governor J.B. Pritzker,
Wednesday, 7 July 2021, at McHenry County College in Crystal Lake, Illinois.
(Official White House Photo by Adam Schultz)

Separating transgender issues from LGBT infrastructure is not
an easy task. All the wealthiest donors have been funding LGB
institutions before they became LGBT-oriented, and only in some
instances are monies earmarked specifically for transgender issues.
Some of these billionaires fund LGBT groups through their myriad
companies, multiplying their contributions many times over in
ways that are also difficult to track.

These funders often go through anonymous funding
organizations such as Tides Foundation, founded and operated by
Pike. Large corporations, philanthropists, and organizations can
send enormous sums of money to the Tides Foundation, specify
the direction the funds are to go, and have the funds get to their
destination anonymously. Tides Foundation creates a legal firewall
and tax shelter for corporations and funds political campaigns,
often using legally dubious tactics.

These men and others, including pharmaceutical companies
and the US government, are sending millions of dollars to LGBT

causes. Overall, reported global spending on LGBT is now estimated at $560 million (from 2017–2018). From 2003–2013, reported funding for transgender issues increased more than eightfold, growing at threefold the increase of LGBT funding overall, which quadrupled from 2003 to 2012. This huge spike in funding happened at the same time transgenderism began gaining traction in American culture.

$560 million is a lot of money. Is it enough to change laws, uproot language and force new speech on the public, to censor, to create an atmosphere of threat for those who do not comply with gender identity ideology?

Transgenderism: A new medical and lifestyle market

It seems obvious now to look at the money behind transgenderism. Many new markets have opened because of it. The first gender clinic for children opened in Boston in 2007. In the past ten years, more than 30 clinics for children with purported gender dysphoria have arisen in the United States alone, the largest serving 725 patients.

Over the past decade, there has been an explosion in transgender medical infrastructure across the United States and world to 'treat' transgender people. In addition to gender clinics proliferating across the United States, hospital wings are being built for specialized surgeries, and many medical institutions are clamoring to get on board with the new developments.

Doctors are being trained in cadaver symposiums across the world in all manner of surgeries related to transgender individuals, including phalloplasty, vaginoplasty, facial feminization surgery, urethral procedures, and more. More and more American corporations are covering transgender surgeries, drugs, and other expenses. Endocrinologists have been seeking the fountain of youth in hormones for more than a generation, and the subsequent earnings for marketing those hormones, remain a quest for gold.

Puberty blockers are another growing market. The plastic surgery arm of medicine is staged for an infusion of cash, also from organ transplants, especially womb transplants for men identifying as women who may want future pregnancies. These surgeries are already being practiced on animals and the first successful womb implant from a deceased female donor to another female has already happened. Biogenetics is poised to be the investment of the future, says Rothblatt, who has headed a massive pharmaceutical corporation and is now heavily invested in biogenetics and transplants.

Transgenderism has certainly made its way into the American marketplace, so it seems important to consider the implications of this as we pass laws regarding transgender individuals' and our civil liberties. Transgenderism sits squarely in the middle of the medical industrial complex which is by some estimates even bigger than the military industrial complex.

With the medical infrastructure being built, doctors being trained for various surgeries, clinics opening at warp speed, and the media celebrating it, transgenderism is poised for growth. LGB people, a once-tiny group of women and men trying to love those of the same sex openly and be treated equally within society, has likely already been subsumed by capitalism and is now infiltrated by the medical industrial complex via transgenderism.

Who works to institutionalize transgender ideology?

Much more important than funds going directly to the LGBT lobby and organizations – only a fraction of which trickles down to assist people who identify as transgender – is the money invested by the men mentioned above, governments, and technology and pharmaceutical corporations to institutionalize and normalize transgenderism as a lifestyle choice. They are shaping the narrative about transgenderism and normalizing it within the culture using their funding methods.

This article will use the Pritzker family as a case study because they are emblematic of how this works. Others funding trans organizations and normalizing transgenderism are channeling funds in the same ways and are invested in the same medical infrastructure. This can hardly be a coincidence when the very thing essential to those transitioning are pharmaceuticals and technology. It is also important to note that though the trans lobby has sewn itself to the LGB umbrella, LGB people as such are not lifelong medical patients.

The Pritzkers are an American family of philanthropic billionaires worth approximately $32.5 billion, whose fortune was gestated by Hyatt Hotels and nursing homes. They now have massive investments in the medical industrial complex.

Examining just a few of the Pritzkers in this article will give you some indication of their reach and influence as a family, especially as regards the transgender project and their relationship to the medical industrial complex. As you read, remember, transitioning individuals are medical patients for life and the Pritzker family are not an anomaly in their funding trajectory or investments in the medical industrial complex.

Jennifer Pritzker

Once a family man and a decorated member of the armed forces, Jennifer Pritzker now identifies as transgender. He has made transgenderism a high note in philanthropic funding through his Tawani Foundation. He is one of the largest contributors to transgender causes and, with his family, an enormous influence in the rapid institutionalization of transgenderism.

Some of the organizations Jennifer owns and funds are especially noteworthy for examining the rapid induction of transgender ideology into medical, legal and educational institutions. Pritzker owns Squadron Capital, an acquisitions corporation, with a focus on medical technology, medical devices, and orthopedic implants, and the Tawani Foundation, a philanthropic organization with a grants focus on gender and human sexuality.

Pritzker sits on the leadership council of the Program of Human Sexuality at the University of Minnesota, to which he also committed $6.5 million over the past decade. Among many other organizations and institutions Pritzker funds are Lurie Children's Hospital, a medical center for gender non-conforming children, serving 400 children in Chicago; the Pritzker School of Medicine at the University of Chicago; a chair of transgender studies at the University of Victoria in Canada (the first of its kind); and the Mark S. Bonham Centre for Sexual Diversity Studies at the University of Toronto. He also funds the American Civil Liberties Union and his family funds Planned Parenthood, two significant organizations for institutionalizing female-erasing language and support for transgender causes. Planned Parenthood also recently decided to get into the transgender medical market.

Jennifer Pritzker funds strategically, as does his family, by giving to universities that become beholden to his ideology, whose students go on to spread gender ideology by writing pro-trans articles in medical journals and elsewhere. Jennifer's uncle and aunt, John and Lisa Pritzker, gave $25 million to the University of California at San Francisco for a center of children's psychiatry. Jennifer likewise funds hospitals and medical schools where the alumni go on to create transgender specialties and LGBT medical centers, even though lesbians, gays, and bisexuals don't need specialized medical services.

Here are several current activities of Pritzker-funded medical school alumni and recipients of Pritzker money.

- James Hekman founded the LGBT medical care center in Lakewood Ohio.
- David T. Rubin sits on the advisory board of Accordant/CVS Caremark, the largest pharmaceutical chain in the United States. CVS acquired Target department stores' pharmacies in 2015. Target, of course, is the site of a major social controversy about unisex bathrooms and is a corporate funder of the trans-pushing Human Rights Campaign activist group.
- Loren Schechter is the author of the first surgical atlas for transgender surgery, author of pro-trans journals, was awarded

for legal advocacy of transgenders, performs reconstructive surgeries, and is director of transfeminine conferences sponsored by World Professional Association of Transgender Health (WPATH). He also performs reconstructive surgeries at Weiss Memorial Hospital in Chicago. Schechter is treasurer of the newly formed United States arm of WPATH (World Professional Association of Transgender Health), USPATH, holding conferences in Los Angeles for surgeons on transgender surgeries.

- Robert Garofalo, a gay man, is director of the St Lurie children's gender clinic, head of the hospital's division of adolescent medicine, and a professor of pediatrics at Northwestern University, which J. B. Pritzker (whom we will meet later) funds.
- Benjamin N. Breyer is chief of urology at San Francisco General Hospital and a professor at the University of California at San Francisco, specializing in transgender surgery.
- Nicholas Matte teaches at the Mark Bonham Centre for Sexual Diversity Studies at the University of Toronto, with a specialty in queer studies. Jennifer Pritzker also funds the Bonham Centre. Matte lectures around the country on transgender issues and espouses the idea that we are not a sexually dimorphic species.
- Mark Hyman is the Pritzker Foundation Chair in functional medicine at the Cleveland Clinic and director of the Cleveland Clinic Center for Functional Medicine. Cleveland Clinic conducted the United States' first uterus transplant.
- Baylor College of Medicine is on the receiving end of the Pritzker School of Medicine's 'pipeline programs' for people studying to be doctors. Baylor is where the nation's first child was born from a uterus transplant as part of an experimental program funding the procedure for ten women in order to develop uterus transplants ultimately health insurance and taxpayers will pay for rather than being relegated to elective infertility treatment.

Jennifer Pritzker has also helped normalize transgender individuals in the military with a $1.35 million grant to the Palm Center, a University of California, Santa Barbara-based LGBT think tank, to create research validating military transgenderism. He has also donated $25 million to Norwich University in Vermont, a military academy and the first school to launch a Naval Reserve Officers' Training Corps program.

Pritzker's funding is not confined to the United States, but reaches other countries via WPATH, in conferences for physicians studying transgender surgery and funding of international universities.

Penny Pritzker

Cousin to Jennifer Pritzker, Penny Pritzker served on President Obama's Council for Jobs and Competitiveness and Economic Recovery Advisory Board. She was national co-chair of Obama for America 2012 and national finance chair of Obama's 2008 presidential campaign. To say she was influential in getting president Obama elected would be an understatement.

As Obama's secretary of commerce, Penny Pritzker helped create the National Institute for Innovation in Manufacturing Biopharmaceuticals (NIIMBL) by facilitating an award of $70 million from the US Department of Commerce, the first funding of its kind. Obama made transgenderism a pet issue of his administration, holding a meeting at the White House (the first ever) for transgenderism.

The administration quietly applied the power of the executive branch to make it easier for transgender people to alter their passports, get cross-sex treatment at Veteran's Administration facilities, and access public school restrooms and sports programs based on gender identity. These are just a few of the transgender-specific policy shifts of Obama's presidency.

George Soros and Tim Gill are two other major transgender movement funders who generated millions of dollars to get Obama elected, and Jon Stryker was one of the top five contributors to Obama's campaign. Under Obama and President George W. Bush, the federal government also funded the Tides Foundation with $82.7 million, which in turn donated $47.2 million to LGBT issues over the last two decades.

Penny Pritzker has funded the Harvard School of Public Health and, with her husband through their mutual foundation, The Pritzker Traubert Family Foundation, is funding early childhood initiatives as well as providing scholarships to Harvard University medical students. The Boston Children's Hospital Gender Management Services wing physicians are all affiliated with Harvard Medical School. Penny Pritzker also sat on the board at Harvard, where student life offices teach students, many of whom go on to lead US institutions, that "there are more than two sexes."

J. B. Pritzker

Penny Pritzker's brother, J. B. Pritzker, is an American venture capitalist, entrepreneur, philanthropist, and business owner. He is co-founder of the Pritzker Group, a private investment firm that invests in digital technology and medical companies, including Clinical Innovations, which has a global presence. Clinical Innovations is one of the largest medical device companies and in 2017 acquired Brenner Medical, another significant medical group offering innovative products in the fields of obstetrics and gynecology.

J. B. Pritzker provided seed funding for Matter, a startup incubator for medical technology based in Chicago. He also sits on the board of directors at his alma mater, Duke University, where they are making advances in cryopreserving women's ovaries.

J. B. was running for governor of Illinois in 2018 – he won and is still governor – and put $25 million into an Obama administration public-private initiative totaling $1 billion for early childhood education. J. B. and his wife, M. K. Pritzker, donated $100 million to Northwestern University School of Law, partly for scholarships and partly for the school's 'social justice' and childhood law work.

We must look at why this is framed as a civil rights issue when the main issues seem to be capital and social engineering. There doesn't seem to be a sphere of influence that is untouched by Pritzker money, from early childhood education and universities to law, medical institutions, LGBT lobby and organizations, politics, and the military. If they were the only ones funding the institutionalization of transgender ideology, they would still be fantastically influential, but they are joined by other exceedingly wealthy, influential white men, who also have ties to the pharmaceutical and medical industries.

Pharma and tech giants all-in for transgender

Along with support by pharmaceutical giants such as Janssen Therapeutics, Johnson & Johnson, Viiv, Pfizer, Abbott Laboratories, Bristol-Myers Squibb, and Boehringer Ingelheim Pharmaceuticals, major technology corporations including Google, Microsoft, Amazon, Intel, Dell, and IBM are also funding the transgender project. In February 2017, Apple, Microsoft, Google, IBM, Yelp, PayPal, and 53 other mostly tech corporations signed onto an amicus brief pushing the US Supreme Court to prohibit schools from keeping private facilities for students designated according to sex.

As these corporations were pushing for transgender bathrooms, they were fighting President Trump's travel ban and immigration policies. In reporting the incidents simultaneously, CNN News made the obvious connection between the corporations' interest in the immigration ban and commerce, quoting a legal brief signed by the companies that said, "It is inflicting significant harm on American business, innovation and growth." It made no such equivalent connection for the corporations' interest in transgender rights. The obvious question would be: "Why do they care?" The obvious answer is money.

It behooves us all to look at what the real investment is in prioritizing a lifetime of anti-body medical treatments for a miniscule part of the population.

Melding these manufactured medical issues with a civil rights frame entails the continuance and growth of the problem. Transgenderism is framed as both a medical problem about the gender dysphoria of children who need puberty blockers and are being groomed for a lifetime of medicalization, and as a brave and original lifestyle choice for adults. Martine Rothblatt suggests we are all transhuman, that changing our bodies by removing healthy tissue and organs and ingesting cross-sex hormones over the course of a lifetime can be likened to wearing make-up, dyeing our hair, or getting a tattoo. If we are all transhuman, expressing that could be a never-ending saga of body-related consumerism.

The massive medical and technological infrastructure expansion for a tiny (but growing) fraction of the population with gender dysphoria, along with the money being funneled into this project by those heavily invested in the medical and technology industries, seems to make sense only in the context of expanding markets for changing the human body. Trans activists are already clamoring for a change from 'gender dysphoria' to 'gender incongruence' in the next revision to the International Classification of Diseases, the ICD-11. [This happened.] The push is on for insurance-paid hormones and surgeries for anyone who believes his or her body is in any way 'incongruent' with his or her 'gender identity'.

Bodily diversity appears to be the core issue, not gender dysphoria; that and unmooring people from their biology via language distortions to normalize altering human biology. Institutionalizing transgender ideology does just this. This ideology is being promoted as a civil rights issue by wealthy white men with enormous influence who stand to personally benefit from their political activities.

It is incumbent upon all of us to look at what the real investment is in prioritizing a lifetime of anti-body medical treatments for a miniscule part of the population, building an infrastructure for them, and institutionalizing the way we perceive ourselves as human beings, before being human becomes a quaint concept of the past.

#2

Big pharma, big tech, and synthetic sex identities[2]

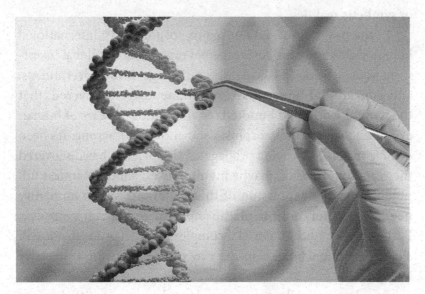

I hope to clarify tonight, what's happening in the name of transgenderism – why it's happening and who is profiting from it.

I began researching this issue because of my alarm at the censorship experienced by those trying to critique it. That was nearly a decade ago. What has emerged for me is a clear indication that we're being manipulated and groomed to accept radical changes to human evolution engineered by those at the highest echelons of society invested in the biotech, pharmaceutical, technological, and financial industries.

First, let's situate ourselves in time.

---

2   Speech given at Hillsdale College, 29 July 2022. <https://freedomlibrary.hillsdale.edu/programs/campus-lectures/big-pharma-big-tech-and-synthetic-sex-identities>

As a species, we're beginning a new stage of human evolution, emerging from the information and digital age. The future will see more developments in human data collection to build greater systems of artificial intelligence and engineering, biotechnology, transhumanism, and the creation of bigger virtual systems of reality or synthetic realities.

In the past decade, all our major corporations, international human rights and non-governmental organizations, global investment houses, banks, medical institutions, legal firms, governments, and educational bodies have simultaneously 'discovered' that the natural world and hundreds of thousands of years of human evolution via sexual dimorphism somehow got it wrong. It's been one *big* mistake. It's being propagated that science has discovered there are hundreds of, maybe infinite, sexes, and to manifest full potential in the expression of these alternate sexes, humanity needs the intervention of the medical industrial complex. Further, the medical industrial complex is so generous that it will silence anyone who gets in the way of its efforts for a diversity of expression.

People, especially politicians, have become terrified to say that women are adult human females, rarely arguing about what men are because that's not up for question. Simultaneously, manipulation of our DNA and CRISPR/Cas9 technology to control the human genome is well underway. Through the use of in-vitro fertilization, embryo and sperm cryopreservation, embryo transfer, sperm injections, surrogacy, and research into artificial wombs, etc., developing technologies are poised to usurp human female reproduction. This is happening in conjunction with women's legal and linguistic erasure to promote a spectrum of sexes. The growth of 'gender clinics' for children will see many children in the next generation sterilized and in need of assisted reproductive technologies if they want to have children.

My research has shown that we are starring in a corporate coup to colonize human sex for profit and to engineer the evolution of humanity. Though this is more believable than the idea that western societies are being overhauled for a fraction of humanity who don't believe they are male or female, we have spent a decade arguing about, and obsessing over, 'gender people'.

The word *transgenderism* is not fit for communication. It does not define anything clearly but obscures the industry manifested in its name. It's an umbrella term with no borders, under which sit too many conflicting ideas, allowing its definitional goalposts to move whenever anyone critiques its ideology and the markets forming around it. Instituting gender identity as a legal concept deconstructs what it means to be human at its core: a biologically, sexually dimorphic species. This is the point. Gender is an obfuscation. The corporate state is deconstructing sex.

One of the uses of the word *transgenderism* is as a rebranding of the word *transsexualism*, which is rooted in transvestic fetishism and is the colloquial term for the paraphilia of autogynephilia, whereby men, aroused at the thought of themselves as females, wear stereotypical women's clothing, specifically undergarments, to satisfy a sexual compulsion. This used to happen in private.

When pharmacology and technology made it possible for the tiny number of men with this fetish to escalate their behaviors to appropriate surgically constructed facsimiles of female biology, or synthetic sex characteristics, transsexualism took root in the medical industry. In 1965, when Johns Hopkins Hospital in Baltimore, Maryland, opened a clinic to manipulate human sex characteristics – the first clinic to do so in the US – it was for experimental reasons, not political ones. It became a model for other clinics, even after closing its doors in 1979 after finding the surgeries were unsuccessful. A 2011 Swedish study, mirroring Johns Hopkins' findings, found that the risk of suicide was much higher for people who'd had surgeries to change their outward sex characteristics versus the general public.

It should also be noted that these genital mutilations were performed on homosexual men because of modern society's intense homophobia. This still occurs in other countries, such as Iran. This is how a paraphilia of adult men has come to be associated with people who are same-sex attracted, though they are radically different experiences. Homosexuality is embodied sexual desire grounded in reciprocity. Autogynephilia is an objectifying, compulsive, and dissociative fetish.

It's 40 years since Johns Hopkins closed its clinic doors, and yet The Gender Mapping Project organization estimates there are now thousands of gender clinics around the world, 400 that offer to medically manipulate the sex of children – often children who don't conform to strict sex-role stereotypes and have been assessed as likely to grow up to be gay. China opened its first clinic in 2021. There are at least two clinics in California that perform what they call 'non-binary' surgeries on men's genitalia, creating a cavity with inverted scrotal skin while leaving the penis intact. They also perform nullification surgeries by removing sex organs entirely.

For this talk, and for the industry side of this issue that I intend to highlight, transsexualism as a paraphilia that compulsively and specifically objectifies female reproductive biology needs a more vital examination. Exacerbated by the escalation of the porn industry and made possible by the growth of powerful technologies tied to profiteering, this fetish of adult men aroused by appropriating synthetic female sex characteristics has created a perfect storm that's manifested into a new industry: the gender industry.

Autogynephilia reduces women's sexed humanity to parts available for purchase, as all aspects of the sex industries do. Support is flourishing for this development under a human rights framework, while women are being erased in language and law, and the men with this paraphilia are given more prominence.

As the technology and pharmaceuticals to perform more realistic synthetic sex surgeries advance, society is forced to accept this paraphilia and accept the ideology that's developed around it, which denies our biological reality, raising us above the natural world, where we are supposed to thrive in a living tapestry.

The 'gender lobby', or the techno-totalitarians as I consider them to be, and their insane assertions that human sex is not binary but exists on a spectrum, are not just a political movement invested in virtuousness run amok. Influential people with money drive this ideology – not just for profit, of which there is plenty – but for engineering human biology toward a transhuman, and eventually a post-human, evolution. *Transhumanism* is the movement of humanity toward a more integral fusion with technologies and artificial intelligence. *Post-humanism* is the transformation of our species into something beyond human. Eventually, or so those working toward this goal hope, we will live in virtual reality without the need for reproductive sex, genetic families, or even food, and women will become obsolete. This ideology is being engineered into children's and young adults' social media and television programs and is taught in their schools. Children and young people are the target market for this new industry and for biotechnological intrusions into their anatomy, which is why they're being taught to dissociate from biological reality and their sexed bodies.

Girls are lining up for elective double mastectomies, thinking they can be boys and creating funding campaigns for their surgeries. Johnson & Johnson – the pharmaceutical giant – markets these surgeries as liberating. In 2018, at the Ronald Reagan Medical Center at the University of California Los Angeles, the Department of Obstetrics and Gynecology advertised several options for young females who think they can be men to have their reproductive organs removed, a procedure termed 'gender affirming care'.

Women are losing the language specific to their biology and are now called *birthing people*, *menstruators*, and *chest feeders* to be 'inclusive' of men. This is dehumanizing, and that's no accident.

Before looking at a few of the key individuals driving the idea that sex exists on a spectrum, and their interconnections within the techno-medical complex and the LGBT non-governmental organizations building the framework of a human rights movement, let's look at the profiteering of the techno-medical complex around creating synthetic sexes regardless of the harms it breeds.

Journalist Sue Donym, reporting on the market in puberty blockers for children, chronicles the cost of Lupron, a drug used to stop children's puberty, compared to its use for treating adult conditions in men and women. Pediatric versions of Lupron are far more expensive than adult versions. Lupron for treating endometriosis in women is $4,800 for a three-month dose, while its pediatric version is $9,700 for the same dose. A subcutaneous implant for delivering the drug to children is $35,000, whereas a subcutaneous adult implant to administer Lupron for the treatment of advanced prostate cancer costs $4,400. And the costs of those drugs run to hundreds of thousands of dollars when children use them for *up to seven years*. That amounts to $9,700 per child every three months for up to seven years, adding up to $270,000 for one patient. If even one hundred children took these drugs for seven years, that's $27 million in drug sales.

Global Market Insights, a research firm, reported on the market for genital surgery for identity purposes, putting 2019 profits at $316 million while projecting a 25% growth rate in surgeries by 2026. This amounts to profits of $1.5 billion for the United States alone. The firm concluded that growth drivers for synthetic sexes are favorable government policies in the United States, where there is greater awareness of surgeries, of technological advancements coupled with increasing effectiveness of the surgeries, and accessibility to sex surgical centers. It should be noted that although these surgeries were created by men, for adult men, the largest demographic selecting these surgeries now are adolescent females. We don't hear much about the demographic of middle-aged women who opt for these surgeries.

Opening markets in sexual identities could have only happened by violating the sex boundary between males and females. The paraphilia of transsexualism, rebranded as 'cool' for today's youth and added to a human rights umbrella of sexual identity, accomplishes this. The market in sex manipulation surgery now has a new consumer base.

The small civil rights movement of lesbians, gays and bisexuals grew into a global purchasing juggernaut once the medical industrial complex infiltrated it during the1980s AIDS crisis.

OUTLeadership, the business networking arm of the LGBT market, currently reports $4.7 trillion in buying power. By 2000, when the AIDS epidemic was brought under control, the two most powerful LGBT non-governmental organizations in America emerged. One was the Gill Foundation, started by billionaire Tim Gill. Gill is an American philanthropist and LGBT rights activist. He was among the first open homosexuals to be on the *Forbes* 400 list of America's richest people. As of 2019, he was the largest individual donor to the LGBT rights movement in US history. Gill is also the founder of the pioneering computer software company Quark. He now owns an artificial intelligence company called Josh.ai.

The second largest LGBT rights NGO in the United States is the Arcus Foundation, founded by Jon Stryker, heir to his family's $133.55 billion (figure updated April 2024) medical supply corporation, Stryker Medical. He funds Arcus Foundation with profits from his stock in Stryker Medical. Jon Stryker is also a founding board member of Greenleaf Trust, a privately owned bank in Kalamazoo, Michigan. Stryker and Gill are not your typical grassroots activists.

Stryker Medical has over 40 subsidiaries in 100 countries around the world. Of the top ten countries outside the US using Stryker Medical supplies, at least eight are hotbeds of gender activism and political pressure driving gender identity laws, including the UK, Ireland, Canada, Germany, the Netherlands and Australia.

North America is home to Stryker Medical and the Arcus Foundation and is its largest consumer base. Their next largest consumer base is the UK, where the Arcus Foundation has another branch at Cambridge University.

Ireland, home to Transgender Equality Network Ireland (TENI), is a boiling cauldron of synthetic sex rights activism. TENI is funded by Transgender Europe, which is heavily funded by the Arcus Foundation (read: Stryker Medical).

Transgender Europe was established in 2005. It has 195 member organizations in 48 different countries. Ireland is home to three branches of Stryker Medical and 19 of the top 20 global pharmaceutical and biopharmaceutical companies.

The Arcus Foundation poses as a human rights organization, but it subsists on the millions generated by Stryker Corporation stock. Jon Stryker has built the political scaffolding to push synthetic sex surgeries as positive human progression and normal human expression – into our cultures, our institutions, our laws, and more importantly and dangerously, the global marketplace via philanthropic funding to LGBT NGOs, universities, churches, sports, legal firms, and other organizations.

Having successfully helped to drive gender ideology in western cultures, the Arcus Foundation is now sowing the seeds for normalizing synthetic sex identities in the global south with millions of dollars in funding to the International Trans Fund (ITF).

Who else in the world besides the American medical industrial complex – by some estimates bigger than the American military industrial complex –could wield so much global power as to have the media, international corporations, global banks, investment houses, the largest law firms in the world, and the armed services do their bidding selling synthetic sex identities?

We must also take seriously the ideology of Martine Rothblatt, a renowned US entrepreneur who identifies as a transsexual and a transhumanist, and who has appropriated the female sex with technology and drugs. He co-founded Sirius Satellite Radio, owns United Therapeutics – a major biopharmaceutical corporation – and worked on the Human Genome Project at the UN level.

Rothblatt was mentored into transhumanism by Ray Kurzweil of Google, and William Sims Bainbridge, another transhumanist, and chief architect of the US government's high-tech boom. Rothblatt created a robot replica of his wife, developed by Hanson Robotics. He has written and spoken about transcending flesh and is a strong presence at OUTLeadership, the business networking arm of the LGBT lobby. He believes transgenderism is an on-ramp to transhumanism, and he created a technological transhumanist religion called Terasem, whose credo is we are making God as we are implementing technology that is *ever more all-knowing, ever-present, all-powerful, and beneficent.* Rothblatt is also a lawyer and the author of the very first gender bill. He worked with several other transsexual lawyers to give a legal structure to physical dissociation from the sexed body. He has written extensively on the need to overhaul our system of labeling people as male or female based on their genitalia, and on the future of creating humans with new reproductive technology. He is now sitting on the board of the Mayo clinic in the US.

It should be noted here that men who fund the current gender industry that sterilizes young people are also invested in the technologies of assisted reproduction. Amazon launched its first fertility center in 2019, partnered with the Maven Clinic in 2023 for more of the same, while the Bezos family invested $166 million, in 2021, in a hospital offering 'gender services' to youth in Brooklyn, N.Y. Marc Benioff, owner of *TIME* magazine, Co-CEO, and Co-Founder of Salesforce, and a pioneer of cloud computing, funds clinics to medicalize children's natural puberty and has simultaneously invested in Overture Life, an embryology lab, making in-vitro fertilization more accessible than ever.

Jennifer Pritzker and his family should not be overlooked in the development of synthetic sex identities. The Pritzkers are one of the richest families in America. They made their fortune founding the Hyatt hotel corporation but have since moved their investments to the techno-medical sector and now push synthetic sex as an identity. The Pritzkers have sent hundreds of millions of philanthropic dollars into educational, medical, cultural, military and legal institutions in America, Canada and Israel, to drive the concept that human reproductive sex exists on a spectrum and is part of the human rights frame for the same-sex attracted. Jennifer Pritzker was born James Pritzker. After marrying and fathering three children, he decided in middle age that he was a woman. He adopted a synthetic female identity and has sent millions of dollars via his philanthropic organization, the Tawani Foundation, to institutionally change our ideas about sex.

Tawani Enterprises, the private investment counterpart of the philanthropic foundation, invests in and partners with Squadron Capital, a Chicago-based private investment vehicle that acquires medical device companies that manufacture instruments for surgical use, mirroring Jon Stryker's trajectory. Jennifer's cousin, Penny Pritzker, who sits on the board of Microsoft, was hugely influential in getting President Obama elected and was later chosen as his Secretary of Commerce. Obama became the first 'trans' president, meeting at the White House with the higher-ups in the LGBT lobby, and he drove bills through the government to support synthetic sex as identity.

In 2019, Illinois governor J. B. Pritzker, Jennifer's cousin and Penny's brother, issued an Executive Order titled *Strengthening Our Commitment to Affirming and Inclusive Schools* to welcome and support children with manufactured sex identities. It established a task force to outline statewide criteria for schools and teachers that recommended districts amend their school board policies "to strengthen protections for transgender, nonbinary, and gender-nonconforming students."

In 2021, Governor Pritzker signed into law a new sex education bill for all public schools in Illinois, the first of its kind designed in accordance with the second edition of the *National Sex Education Standards* to update sex ed curricula in K–12 schools. The bill will be implemented on 1 August 2022. *National Sex Education Standards*, which teach children about gender ideology and the medical manipulation of children's sex for identity purposes, were funded by the Grove Foundation, whose fortune comes from the now-deceased Andrew Grove, a former CEO of Intel Corporation.

Visions of transhumanism and a post-humanity where we fuse with AI might be the reason new legal rights are demanded by those who promote synthetic sexes. Robots and AI don't have a reproductive system. They are assigned synthetic sexes when they are created, which mimics the language of gender identity ideology.

Chile passed a law last year to protect the rights of genetically modified humans, the first country to do so. The world's first two genetically modified babies, Lulu and Nana – 'manufactured' by Chinese scientist He Jiankui – were born in Hong Kong in 2018.

The tech sector supports the synthetic sex industry by funding various LGBT organizations and using their collective financial weight as a threat to change policies.

In 2017, our major tech organizations, including Apple, Intel, Amazon, Google, Salesforce, Tumblr, Twitter, and Yahoo, filed an amicus brief to support synthetic sex identities at the expense of boys' and girls' rights to physical privacy in public bathrooms. Google recently funded the largest LGBT youth organization in the USA, the Trevor Project, with millions of dollars to build an artificial intelligence system. The Trevor Project is also partnered with Astellas Pharmaceutical, makers of puberty-blocking drugs.

As well, the tech sector is highly invested in the development of augmented humans and synthetic realities.

Beyond Ray Kurzweil's Singularity, Elon Musk created the first neural implant device for humans, called Neuralink, to help people navigate computers with their minds. Mark Zuckerberg has his own brand of virtual reality system, called Metaverse. Yuval Harari, working closely with Klaus Schwab at the World Economic Forum, is considered one of the world's most influential public intellectuals. He believes the most important challenges facing the world are technological disruption, ecological collapse, and nuclear threat. He thinks that within a few decades, or a couple of centuries at most, humanity will upgrade itself into a different type of species through our technological advances. He also makes the connections between synthetic sex identities and transhumanism and speaks about a coming virtual reality for humans overlaid on the biosphere. We have become compulsively addicted to that which does not reciprocate and the rapid advancement of fetishes to express our sexuality is representative of this.

Humans are connected to the biosphere by sex. The deconstruction of sex in language and law, its separation from intimacy via fetish and porn, and the manipulation of young people's sex characteristics, seem to pave the way for further encroachments into our biology and our more complete melding with technology. Synthetic sexes work as a grooming process for the public to accept more violations of our physical boundaries while also providing young, healthy, resilient bodies to experiment on.

Putting these developments into the context of unfettered corporatism, an economic system that pursues profit like a heat-seeking missile that is destroying the planet, treating our home like a bottomless well of resources to feed itself, it appears that humanity is next in line for colonization.

Our technologies, sutured to this market, have created glorious cathedrals of civilization, but the planet's coral reefs are disappearing, and there are Texas-sized islands of plastic in the oceans that we don't know what to do with. We have obliterated and tortured so many other species to grow our magnificent technologies, and the radioactive waste at Fukushima is still growing. Currently, millions of mega tons of it are being dumped into the ocean. Our planet's water has been poisoned and sold back to us in plastic bottles that wind up as gyres in the ocean. We have extraordinary towers of learning that are teaching the next generation that allowing this system to devour them, too, is the zenith of freedom.

The market has finally come for humans, dressed up as 'gender expression', with its eye on our genetic codes. Gender ideology opens the door. The market is standing there dressed to the nines, and we're inviting it in for a full-course meal. It will probably be our last – unless we can understand what we're looking at and use whatever free will we have left to organize and resist synthetic sex identities, institutionally, legally, and politically.

#3

Capitalism, the new, new left and the gender industry: Diversity and inclusion are corporate speak for homogenization and totalitarianism[3]

Inclusivity is more than a social cause, it's a business opportunity. It's time to maximize your business growth.

—DMI Consulting

Let me get this out of the way, because it seems more than a few people still need to hear this. CORPORATIONS DO NOT CARE ABOUT YOU!

'Diversity and inclusion' (D and I) comprise a new business mantra. Programs and language based on the normalization of body dissociation are being corporately cultivated around the world. The programs being instituted appeal to our emotions, to entice us to believe that companies care about people and just want to create one big happy, diverse work-family, which includes marginalized sectors of society – most notably those who imagine they have a sex (gender is used as a euphemism) that is not male or female. The overlooked are finally being given a place at the table!

Or are they?

The new, new liberal left in America, the left that has emerged out of a traditional new left which cared about the working class, blacks and women's rights, who yearned for a more equal and just social order, is unrecognizable to many of us who've long been of the traditional left. That left, just a decade ago, sparked a potentially revolutionary movement on Wall Street, calling out the financial industry and the monopolies ruining our lives and our planet.

---

3   First published 21 September 2021. <https://www.the11thhourblog.com/post/capitalism-the-new-new-left-and-the-gender-industry>

Emerging out of the carcass of that potentially revolutionary movement is a left that has recently climbed into bed with those same big banks. Snuggled up in bed with them, fluffing their pillows, are Big Pharma and Big Tech. The left is running around screaming at protests, getting comprehensive media coverage, silencing voices in our universities and institutions, and shouting loudly that people claiming their sex is not male or female need human rights. These manufactured sexes are supported by, promoted, and advertised by Big Pharma, Big Tech, and Big Banking. This new, unrecognizable left sees no irony at all in their behavior.

These purported new sexes, ostensibly requiring special human rights, depend on a narrative that sexual dimorphism isn't real, that it exists on a spectrum of sexes.

This is the gender industry, and with projected profit margins reaching into the billions by 2026 for surgeries on healthy sex organs alone and the amount of advertising curated to sell it, it is going to be very profitable indeed.

How has the left been so duped about new markets being manifested out of sex that they scream liberation every time someone dares to mention the glaring inconsistency of human rights for corporate profiteering off young adults' and children's bodies?

The left knows corporations do not care about the color of our skin, whether we are oppressed because of the said color of our skin, whether we live in an igloo or a cardboard box, whether the icebergs are melting, or whether the Fukushima nuclear plant is dumping millions of metric tons of radioactive waste into the oceans, externalizing the cost of doing business. How do they not understand that corporations do not care about anybody's identity? Unless those identities are opening markets.

The constant business-woke-posing D and I for Black Lives Matter (BLM), the LGBT Inc., and the often-corporate mixing of both under the 'Black Trans Lives Matter' slogan is about profit. Every little advertising slogan, every word, is carefully selected to appeal to an ever-increasing fragmentation of humanity into subcategories to be marketed to. It is all about the corporate bottom line. If they can convince us that the disembodiment movement of 'gender identity' is akin to the civil rights movement for black Americans or has anything to do with LGBs, they've roped us into their narrative of care. Further, if they can convince more black Americans of their insane narrative of dissociation-from-sexed-reality-as-progress, it supports the illusion they are selling to all of us. Fortunately, that isn't going well so far. Despite their efforts to corral black youth and the relentless corporate propaganda aimed at them, black youth are not crying about their 'gender identities' or clamoring for cross-sex hormones.

Police at Occupy Wall Street, New York City, 21 June 2018

The left knows corporations don't care. The working class knows this too. It's why the Occupy Wall Street movement evolved so quickly. I was there, a decade ago, at ground zero, with 40,000 people from every walk of life, as we traversed the Brooklyn Bridge in protest of the choke hold the financial sector had on us. Now, these same people are waving flags in traditional baby-colored pink, blue and white, screaming about human emancipation through medical identities. Many stitched themselves to the techno-medical complex for life.

For a concise and readily comprehensible explanation of how capitalism functions, I urge you to examine the work of Stephanie McMillan, a lifelong activist and an anti-capitalist. She explains, in language that is entirely accessible, how corporations are set up to compete in the global marketplace: "To care about people over profits would jeopardize the corporatist's position within that system and their livelihood." Corporate heads consist of those with the most significant wealth who depend on an exploited working class not just to function, but to suck wealth upward from the bottom, creating ever more wealth for a few, leaving the masses at the bottom with less and less. This is a worse crisis for women worldwide, who, according to UN statistics, put in 12.5 billion hours of unpaid care work each day – thus contributing at least $10.8 trillion annually to the global economy. However, the reporting of these statistics will no longer be an accurate measure of what is transpiring globally since men will be included in the stats for women under the new corporate gender regime.

We are living in an oligarchic gulag, one that isn't very private. Our communities are being opened to the acceptance and normalization of a male fetish based on dissociation from sexed reality, creating a sexual psychodrama of our corporate and civil landscapes – for profit – while dismembering people and creating more identities to market to.

Because we are governed by corporate monopolies and the billionaires behind them, driving a steady stream of propaganda through our media, we no longer know what fake news is and what real news is. We don't know what men and women are (or we pretend not to, to fit in). We don't know if people on social media or advertising are real or computer generated, and our ability to speak about anything outside the corporately generated illusions plaguing us is being penalized in myriad ways, not the least of which is controlled and censored speech. Yet suddenly, we are to believe, and many on the new, new liberal left do, that these monstrous monopolies that have ravaged an entire planet have suddenly changed their ways and care about people. They primarily care about these new imaginary sexes being manufactured out of technology-driven propaganda, philanthropic funding, corporate cash, and the techno-medical complex.

Will Meyer, in a recent issue of *Business Insider*, gives us a look at the corporate hypocrisy posing as care about the marginalized. He reports that:

> IBM and Microsoft claimed they would no longer sell facial recognition software to law enforcement, signaling their alignment with the Soros-backed BLM movement, despite both corporations remaining deeply invested in punitive systems that continue to harm Black and brown lives.

The BLM movement has the same capitalists behind it as the gender industry.

Selling D and I to the public is such a big business that there are corporations that teach other companies how to market it effectively. This fracturing of humanity, via the colonization of human sex, is how capitalism functions. It splits everything into smaller and smaller fragments to open markets. Where we once had a single family physician to help us heal, we now have a plethora of specialists to treat everything from lung cancer to toenail fungus. Where we have had a sexually dimorphic species, we now have medical identities that deconstruct sex being foisted upon us, to open markets, to engineer society and humanity.

Those with wealth create more wealth for themselves, while underlings, not having access to wealth, land, or goods, are forced to sell their labor for less and less money. The wealth, goods, and land are all siphoned off by the corporatists. Well, now the corporatists, with little left to extract, have come for human sex, and they are not leaving until they have it, unless we rise in resistance and reclaim what is left after their ravaging.

#4

The gay rights movement has been hijacked by a radical transhumanist agenda[4]

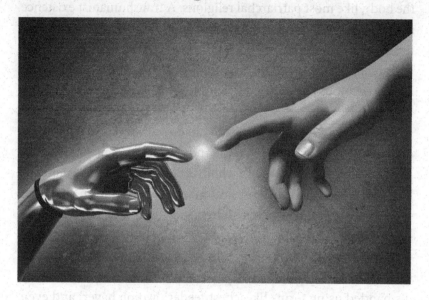

Western societies are in the vortex of Transhumanism. We are being sucked in because this radical transhumanist agenda and its eugenicist underpinnings are obscured by a popular LGB human rights veneer.

'Transgenderism' is a word acting as a social bridge between transsexualism and transhumanism. It is an umbrella term with weak borders that allows this bridging quality to transhumanism to nimbly evade scrutiny. Transsexualism is primarily an adult male fetish that compulsively objectifies and covets womanhood. Men with autogynephilia (the professional name for this form of transsexualism) seek to medically appropriate the sexed humanity

---

4 First published 19 October 2022 in *Reality's Last Stand*. <https://www.realitys laststand.com/p/the-gay-rights-movement-has-been>

of women by purchasing surgical simulacrums of their sexed reality in parts to assuage their compulsion.

Transhumanism is the movement to increase human lifespan and cognition through a more intimate melding with technology, artificial intelligence, and biotechnology. The transhumanist agenda sees immortality as its ultimate end goal and splits the mind from the body, like most patriarchal religions. A transhumanist existence is one where biological reality, such as the border between male and female, would become irrelevant. Through virtual reality and fusion with technology, reproductive sex would become obsolete, and having sex would be reduced to a mind game, with our corporeality left behind.

The word 'transgenderism' obscures the escalation of a compulsive sexual fetish into the industry forming around it, an industry that erases women's wholly sexed humanity in language, law, and all our institutions, and markets dissociation from the sexed body as progressive to children and youth. It is the apex of the sex industries, reducing women to parts for commercial and sexual use. Women only exist as parts to be consumed or commercially used for their reproductive capacities. Women are systematically dismantled using terms like 'chest feeder', 'womb haver', and even 'surrogate'.

Transhumanist philosophy has been with us since at least 1957, coined by the British philosopher Julian Huxley, grandson of the prominent biologist T. H. Huxley, a brother of novelist Aldous Huxley who wrote *Brave New World*. *Brave New World* was published in 1932 and anticipated vast scientific advancements in reproductive technology, sleep-learning, psychological manipulation, and classical conditioning combined to make a dystopian society. Julian Huxley was a committed eugenicist. His post-Second World War eugenic thinking was a crucial overpass from what has been referred to as old eugenics to new eugenics based on molecular biology, which can be likened to the bridge from transsexual operations to transhumanism: from experimenting on human sexual characteristics to manipulating human genetic codes and beyond.

Eugenics is the study of arranging human reproduction to create more 'desirable' characteristics, and the forced sterilization of those with 'undesirable' elements. Though the old eugenics has been discredited as unscientific and racially biased because of the adoption of its tenets by the Nazis to justify their treatment of Jews, disabled people, and other minority groups, eugenics hasn't gone away. It has simply advanced with technology and is riding the tsunami wave of unfettered corporatism. It is now coming at us through transhumanism and genetic engineering. Eugenics has a long and complex history that cannot be tackled here, but the current experiments on children's healthy bodies and sex organs, many of whom are likely to grow up to be gay or lesbian, and many who also have autism and other mental health problems, echo its tenets. These 'transgender' experiments sterilizing young people are currently being forwarded under the rainbow banner of 'human rights'.

'Transgenderism', a word first used in 1965 by psychiatrist John F. Oliven in his book *Hygiene and Pathology*, was used to denote a transsexual's desire that leaped beyond the compulsive urge to dress in culturally sanctioned women's clothing to appropriating their secondary sex characteristics through surgeries and hormones. Transvestic fetishism became transsexualism, though some men did not opt for surgeries and simply continued to cross-dress.

'Transgenderism' is an offshoot of both these terms and is being used to rebrand transsexualism to appeal to a new, youthful market. It is a harbinger of the genetic and technological manipulations we are conditioned to accept via transhumanism obscured by co-opting the familiar branding of a wildly successful human rights movement. It is an anti-human agenda.

The next most crucial step toward the transhumanist goal is to usurp human reproduction and move it into the tech sector. The assisted reproductive market is currently $27.3 billion and is projected to reach $41.4 billion by 2030. This market is being invested in by some of the same elites investing in the gender industry, who are invested in the medical and tech sectors in general, and who are simultaneously using the LGB human rights political infrastructure to abolish sexual dimorphism: reproductive sex. It's a perfect fit because individuals in same-sex relationships will need the assisted fertility market if they wish to reproduce – and only those with considerable resources can finance these risky medical procedures. The rest will stand as the medical 'refuse' of eugenicists, sterilized for life.

The first 'gender bill' was cultivated by a group of men with transvestic fetishism in the early '90s. At least one of these men, Martine Rothblatt, has undergone transsexual surgery, a misnomer since no one can change their sex. He is a transhumanist (no one has yet transitioned from human either), owns a major biopharmaceutical company, a xenotransplantation farm for harvesting animal organs to transplant into humans, a 3D organ printing corporation, and has created a robot of his wife Bina. Rothblatt worked on the Human Genome Project at the UN level and created a technological religion called Terasem. He is the co-creator of Sirius XM satellite radio. Rothblatt is highly renowned in technology, political, and business circles. He has written about the necessity of overriding the process of categorizing men and women by their biology and believes that sexual dimorphism is tantamount to South African Apartheid. He has also written extensively on the future of reproduction via technology and transgressing our species' boundaries.

Rothblatt was tutored into transhumanism by Ray Kurzweil of Google, a company investing in the gender industry on various fronts while it collects our data.

In a 2015 report from *The Atlantic*, Rothblatt discusses gene editing, the rights of human cyborgs, human data collection, synthetic genomics, and the coming age of pharmacogenomics – treating people with drugs that align with their genes – and bioinformatics – an interdisciplinary field that develops methods and software tools for understanding biological data.

While what is happening with the term 'transgenderism' is the attempt to override our species' sex, transhumanism is an attempt to breach the limits of our species' mortality via technology and biotechnology. Both concepts would be a tough sell to the mainstream public, who remain mostly unaware of the enormous leaps in technology that have been made toward engineering humanity out of our roots in the biosphere and toward a more intimate fusing with technology and biotechnology. 'Transgenderism' is the bridge to get us there because it is a disorienting term without strict meaning whose goalposts constantly move to include new ideas, even as they contradict what has already been suggested. It is, in essence, transhumanism being buoyed and obscured by LGBs, whom they eventually seek to dismantle along with the rest of us.

Trangenderism/transhumanism is being forced into every sector of society, government, and even into children's schools where they are taught that they can be boys or girls as they choose; it is a bridge to get us to a place of social acquiescence to these changes. This grooming process would be impossible without the LGB civil rights political apparatus and the already culturally cultivated acceptance of homosexual people.

There are conferences all over the world on transhumanism. There are college courses, centers of study, and books, and if you Google 'transhumanism', you will get in the neighborhood of six million hits. The author of the first gender bill is a transhumanist who lectures widely and openly about the connections between the two. Rothblatt has a strong presence at OUTLeadership, the business networking arm of the so-called 'LGBTQ+' community and is affiliated with various hospitals that assault human sex under the guise of 'gender affirming' treatment, including UCLA and Johns Hopkins. He is now on the board of the Mayo Clinic. Zoltan Istvan, a transhumanist, ran for president. Ray Kurzweil, an advisor of Google, one of our most influential technology corporations, is a transhumanist who mentored Martine Rothblatt. OUTLeadership intersects with all our major corporations cross-marketing their $4.7 trillion consumer base to them.

There are men in the highest echelons of politics, technology, education, medicine, sports, Hollywood, and elsewhere, being given platforms to sell us on 'transgenderism'. They have not come up with one coherent definition to help anyone understand it, or why it has gained such prominence and captured the attention of the most influential law firms, international banks, investment houses, governments, corporations, and all our western institutions rapidly and simultaneously. They sell their ideology to the next generation by indoctrinating them in schools against most parents' wishes.

Without the banner of human rights, the transhumanist boat would sink like a stone. It uses vulnerable children as fodder for the coming revolution in assisted fertility to force our trajectory as a species away from the biosphere and further into technology – unless we stop them.

#5

Gender ideology, technology and sexual trauma – a perfect transhumanist storm[5]

I began researching the gender industry a decade ago, specifically the money behind promoting body dissociation as a progressive new lifestyle. It is becoming apparent to many now that medically assaulting children's reproductive organs will go down in history as one of the greatest scandals of all time. What is still escaping most people is the connection this medical assault on children's reproductive organs has to technology; how we are all being systematically, sexually traumatized, and conditioned to dissociate from ourselves by technology. This dissociation is a necessary prelude to a transhumanist paradigm, where tech czars hope to create humans more integrally enmeshed with AI, and the medical industrial complex hopes to profit from these fusions.

We must examine why most adults are unable to respond effectively to the overt exposure of children to extreme sexual material and acts. Why is the brutalization of their sex organs being framed as a human right conflated with same-sex attraction and why don't more adults respond to this atrocity?

Pride Parades have become a public arena for open displays of kink, fetish, and naked adults performing lewd acts for children and adults alike, where disowning one's sex is celebrated. Gender ideology allies, like Peter Tatchell in the UK, promote the dissolution of all sex boundaries as human progress and 'queer liberation'.

Why are the dissolutions of sex boundaries promoted as progress for human society and framed as equality? Who does this serve?

---

5   First published 20 August 2023. <https://jbilek.substack.com/publish/posts/detail/136251088?referrer=%2Fpublish%2Fpos>

Grown men in women's underwear and clown make-up, twerking at children while singing about inclusivity, have been showing up in various venues, including library programs called 'drag queen story hour', since at least 2015. In the US, the first drag queen story hour was performed in San Francisco, the same year Bruce Jenner appeared on the cover of *Vanity Fair* Magazine, claiming womanhood for himself. The venues claim to celebrate diversity, but in fact market dissociation from sexed reality as inclusive of all LGBT people. What does this have to do with the rights of people who are same-sex attracted? Some parents have protested these events, while the media frames them as harmless, often falsely teaming the events with the struggle for the civil rights of black people to cultivate acceptance.

Other parents stand clapping and cheering this assault on their children. What could possess them to do so? In 2021, in another library in the UK, there were grown men wearing rainbow-colored monkey suits, their plastic dildo penises bouncing around with their monkey antics, exposing their naked buttocks to children. All this was embraced as part of the new normal.

The violation of children's psyches happening everywhere is a direct mirror to the violation of our own. The absolute demolition of any sense of modesty or privacy being exhibited on our tech platforms and on theirs, as well as in their schools, is striking. It is such a dangerous precedent being set. As it is wed to greater tech developments, we become more imprisoned, panopticon style. We can go on the internet and see any number of insane things freely – and for free (free, if you don't consider the cost of the data mining for AI and the trauma of sensory overload).

Any child with a phone, tablet or computer, can do the same – and they do. This is what is 'wrong' with them. 'Gender dysphoria' denotes a dissociation from one's sexed reality. Traumatic dissociation is a given when someone is being sexually assaulted.

Children's schools have been invaded with this body-denying ideology of gender identity, driven by special interests and big money, teaching them they can be male or female. First graders are being taught how to masturbate and to not allow their parents to hug them. Many parents are terrified to speak out. Four hundred pediatric sex control clinics have emerged in America, in a decade, to medicalize children's healthy bodies with powerful, off-label drugs. Their puberty is being aborted. They are being sterilized. It's not that no one knows this is happening, though LGBT NGOs have worked by stealth to add the T+, and create organizations that drive the normalization of body dissociation globally.

Children's castration and dismemberment of their sex is national entertainment fodder on reality TV, YouTube, Twitter, Facebook, other social media platforms (read: tech), and mainstream media (read again: tech). YouTube (which encompasses most of the world's entertainment) is owned by Google, the first company to create a transhumanist culture at work. Google wants to give us all augmented reality. Including children. In 2019, it invested $1.5 million in an AI platform for kids with a grant to The Trevor Project, already receiving $37 million in funding. The platform teaches them they can transgress the boundaries of sexed reality with technology, while purportedly saving LGBT kids from suicide.

How is it we are so 'transfixed'? Is our lack of outrage and inaction the result of a technologically induced trauma, sexual and otherwise? Are we dissociating as a response to the abuse we are not even clear we are experiencing? If so, is it a surprise that children do it too?

It seems likely that adults are being manipulated and trauma-tized by the same technological systems overtaking our children, the same all-pervasive techno-medical complex (Big Pharma as it intersects with Big Tech) driving the dissociating ideology of 'gender identity' (GI).

Our trauma is created by a lack of privacy, constant surveillance (we were warned by Edward Snowden and others, and most of us have yet to respond), an addiction to technology, and the vast amount of violence and sexual material we are exposed to via that tech. We are subjected to massive and mounting atrocities, not just in our neighborhoods, but thanks to technology and the internet, all over the world.

Too many adults are exposed to deeply disturbing and violent pornography. Pornhub (read: tech) gets more visits than Netflix or Amazon. Fetishes and sexual encounters based on disconnection and dissociation are being normalized. So much so that today's music videos are far more sexually explicit that yesterday's porn. Today's dark corner porn is violent, composed of vile sexual humiliation and degradation.

According to Professor Gail Dines, who has researched the porn industry for decades, it has to be for men to get off, because the way porn works on the brain, it must become more extreme as the viewer becomes desensitized. Dines calls it "the public health crisis of the digital age." Too many of us also face sustained financial instability and a lack of community. These changes have been growing in ferocity, especially since the COVID pandemic, and leave us unsteady, desperate, confused, and unmoored from reality. We are, in a word, dissociated.

Tack on the recent and rapid deconstruction of sexual dimorphism in language and law, the dismantling of our social structures organized around our sexual dimorphism, unhealthy symbiosis with technology, environmental instability, and unfathomable corruption at every front of politics, media, and society, and is it any wonder we are dissociating on a mass scale? Trauma will do this. We wed ourselves more and more to this rapacious system even as it is destroying us. No wonder we can't help our children. We can't help ourselves.

The idea of a 'gender identity' promotes body dissociation at its most fundamental level. It is not a phenomenon that has just occurred, it has been actively cultivated by the techno-medical complex for which the LGBT NGOs have become a front and from where gender identity ideology and gender identity emerged.

Our youth are being sexually traumatized because the most common response to sexual trauma is body dissociation. They are being bombarded with sexually violent images via internet porn, where they are observers and coerced into performing on tech platforms. 'Trans' cartoon characters sing to them from their childhood programs sporting double mastectomy scars, and sexually explicit material is seeping into their classrooms. They spend more and more time online, just like the adults surrounding them, oblivious of the high-tech marketing and propaganda they are exposed to, by companies that are interfacing with venture capital firms and supporting other tech and medical venues. These are market-driven changes fueled by rapid technological advancements, biopharmaceuticals, and rich men who seek to engineer human evolution – the men spearheading and supporting transhumanist and 'transgender' agendas and who have sewn a body-denying ideology into the market.

Once tied to our institutions and the global economy, body dissociation, seen as positive, runs like a machine set in motion, with no driver.

There are thousands of young people on YouTube and TikTok talking about their dismemberment surgeries, alongside doctors selling dismemberment surgeries. This is more than a fad.

We have got to come out of the trance we are in and face the truth of what is happening to us as a species and what is happening to our children. We are too tied into a technological structure that is destroying our ability to think and respond to this abuse. Our children are being fed into the meat grinder of the vast techno-medical complex, bioengineering our melding to technology. This system which is stitched into a now totalitarian market will stop for no one. Unless we make it stop. First, we must wake up from the trance that technology has us in.

#6
The synthetic sex industry and LGBT Inc. creating a market for big fertility[6]

'Transgender surge' and 'gender affirming care' are euphemisms that are at once political and commercial. They are used to sell the products of synthetic sexes and simultaneously an ideology that supports the products of synthetic sexes while obscuring the business end of things. For many people who support this industry, the marketing of a medical assault on healthy human sex rarely registers because synthetic sexes have been sold to society as a human rights movement, as part of the LGBT. At least two thirds of this cohort of people, like those being sterilized through synthetic

6   First published 14 May 2023.<https://jbilek.substack.com/p/the-synthetic-sex-industry-and-lgbt?utm_source=%2Fsearch%2FThe%2520synthetic%2520sex%2520industry&utm_medium=reader2>

sex surgeries and drugs, will not be able to have their own children without technologically assisted reproduction.

In 2020, the propaganda marketing campaign for synthetic sexes had only been in full operation for six years. The global market in synthetic sex surgeries was still in its infancy, worth only $319 million, according to Global Market Insights, a market research platform supported by the Better Business Bureau. In 2020, the projected growth value of these surgeries for the Medical Industrial Complex (MIC), was $1.5 billion by 2026. These statistics were provided by Market Watch, a website that provides financial information, business news and analysis. It is owned by Dow Jones and Company.

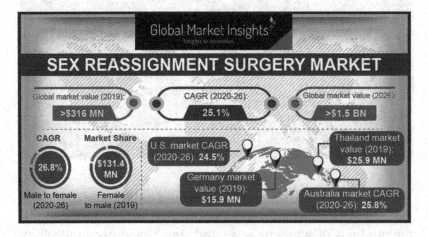

Global Market Insights' statistics state that the market nearly doubled from $319 million in 2020, to $623 million in 2022. They project profits of $1.9 billion for the MIC by 2032, which seem low if they doubled in two years.

In 2023, Market Watch provided another profit projection of $5 billion by 2030. A third profit projection by Future Wise Research, another market research platform in the UK that is also supported by the Better Business Bureau, reports revenue streams of $30 billion by 2028 for the MIC, for these same surgeries. What could account for this vast variation in statistics, and/or the astronomical rise in projected growth, from $1.5 billion by 2026 to $5 billion, and/or $30 billion by 2028–2030?

What is clearly stated in both reports is that synthetic sex surgeries market growth is on the rise and this is attributed to favorable government policies. Other key factors include accessibility and availability of synthetic sex surgery centers, and the rise of awareness worldwide of these surgeries.

'Gender clinics' for youth did not emerge in the US until 2007 and have been growing exponentially since.

What is being called 'gender dysphoria', a body dysmorphia about one's sexed reality, is not a widespread medical problem. It is a widespread propaganda problem. If you live in America, home of Big Pharma, you will have been exposed to a near 24-hour, 365-day-a-year, propaganda marketing Blitzkrieg for these surgeries over the past decade.

In 2014, a black actor, Roderick Laverne Cox, a man with a penchant for wearing women's clothing and synthetic facsimiles of their biology, was positioned on the cover of *TIME* magazine, announcing a 'transgender tipping point'. Since then, the propaganda marketing for a marginalized sector of people with body dysmorphia who need our protection and sympathy, have been fed to us consistently. Vast swaths of this population have now been won over to a denial of reality about biological sex, and others are going along to get along.

In 2015, Bruce Jenner, an icon of American manhood and virility, posed on the cover of *Vanity Fair*. Winner of American Gold at the Montreal Olympics in the triathlon division against the Russians in 1976, he posed in a woman's corset and claimed he'd always been a woman. He was hailed as a new American hero, even after joking about how he had been caught on camera raiding his daughter's underwear drawer.

In 2016, *TIME* magazine followed up from the Cox cover with a spread about a pregnant woman, calling her a man. In 2021, the actress Ellen Page would also grace the cover of *TIME* as 'Eliot'. Every major mainstream media did a coming out story of 'Eliot' and it was *TIME*'s first 'trans man' cover story. This coincided with a *New York Magazine* cover and a disturbing story about a mentally unstable woman and 'her penis'. In the past decade, the marketing of synthetic sexes as progressive has been prolific to say the least. Just google 'Transgender covers', and click 'images', for a taste of the deluge.

The 2023 Market Watch figures for MIC profits from Future Wise Research do not record revenue from removing sex characteristics (nullo surgeries), or the building of synthetic sex characteristics while leaving one's actual sexed anatomy in place ('non-binary' surgeries).

Neither of the Market Watch reports include the sales of puberty blockers. If you have one hundred children on puberty blockers for seven years, the MIC takes in $27 million. Puberty blockers are most often followed by wrong sex hormones to bring the body into submission with the ultimate desired result: an adult body that can pass as the opposite sex. Wrong sex hormones must be taken for life, at an approximate cost of $1500 a month, if a person wants to continue denying the reality of their sexed body. If only one hundred people took cross-sex hormones for twenty years, the profits for the MIC would amount to $36 million. According to the UCLA Williams Institute, there are currently 700,000 children and young people identifying as 'transgender' in the US, showing a sharp rise over the past five years.

The Market Watch figures don't account for other drugs, supplies and services that will be needed for these procedures, when calculating revenue for the MIC. These include anesthesia, antibiotics, anti-rejection drugs, surgical equipment, robotic imaging equipment, special training, research, psychiatric care, 'gender specialists', etc. Further, many people who have these surgeries go on to desire more surgeries to force their bodies into a somewhat passable equivalent of the opposite sex. These can include multiple facial feminization surgeries, shaving the jaw line, tracheal shaving, clavicle shortening surgery to minimize the shoulders, minimization surgeries for the brow line and the feet, and hair implants and hair removal. The profits reported by Market Watch, for the MIC, also don't account for physical complications, a risk which goes with any surgery, and is magnified by surgeries that are new and go against the body's instincts to fix permanent wounds that are created by these surgeries (inverted penis skin into a constructed cavity must be dilated daily to stay open). They don't account for the detrimental effects of using drugs long term and having surgeries on healthy bodies that will have negative reactions as the people who have them age.

US citizens, and those following in our footsteps, are the ones who bear the costs of this propaganda-marketing campaign, economically and socially. Synthetic sex identities sell youth a false promise of liberation by attempting to medically hijack nature – and they are buying its dream. If they survive the mental anguish of internally navigating a lie about who and what they are, the disappointment and regret they will feel when they wake up from the dream, is going to be costly for everyone.

This is not a passing phenomenon. The MIC advertises these surgeries and profits from them. A propaganda campaign, the likes of which we've never seen, is being obscured by the narrative of a human rights movement. Our propaganda apparatus far surpasses anything Edward Bernays, the father of public relations, could have dreamed up because technology is more powerful and much more prominent in our lives than when Bernays was alive.

The manipulation of the American mind has been so absolute we are teetering on the edge of mass hallucination. The marriage of the MIC propaganda marketing apparatus with a social justice movement for same-sex attracted individuals was political genius. This small civil rights movement was hijacked by Big Pharma during the AIDS crisis and created a new specialized consumer. Gay clubs, bookstores, cruises, lawyers, towns and non-governmental organizations emerged to provide a sense of community for a small percentage of the population. It quickly morphed into a juggernaut of cross-marketing political power. If your corporation supported LGB, then LGB would use your corporation.

No longer were LGBs on the fringe of society. Still, with the dissipation of AIDS as a medical problem in the US, and a huge loss of revenue for the MIC from drug sales pertaining to this community, something had to be done. Enter men with a fetish for being women (transsexuals). Changing your 'gender' (read: sex characteristics) would open markets in sex identity in a way that could not happen with only the reality of our two human sexes being visible. LGB was a dead-end marketing stream, until they added the 'T+'.

Surgeries and medical interventions to manifest synthetic sex identities have also opened markets beyond the MIC. There are now 'non-binary' make-up lines, packers for children, special modeling agencies, summer camps, coaching on how to perform the opposite sex, photographs and art of 'special beings', books about these special beings, legal experts to secure their rights. There is now an entire industry that has been coaxed out of unicorn dust by opening markets in synthetic, medical, sex identities.

The LGB human rights veneer for a predatory MIC takes an even darker turn when we understand that lesbians and gays, along with the children being sterilized under their banner of human rights, will all be future consumers of reproductive technology, manifesting as a modern family, created by using women's bodies as technological reproduction factories which would account for women's current linguistic and legal erasure within western societies. The first order of industrial exploitation is to dehumanize the population you intend to exploit.

It's significant that Marc Benioff, the co-creator of Salesforce Cloud Computing Corporation is also the owner of *TIME* magazine, which initiated America to a 'transgender tipping point'. The UCLA gender clinic in California bears his name and he is making big investments in the fertility market. He is, of course, not alone. Jeff Bezos is another billionaire investing heavily in the fertility market. His family has given $166 million to a Brooklyn hospital that provides extensive 'gender care'. I have written broadly about the Pritzker family and their funding machinations to drive 'gender ideology'. Governor Pritzker signed a legislation package in 2021 which updates the state's infertility insurance laws to cover those with synthetic sex identities.

Infertility is currently big business, and the MIC is sterilizing a generation of young people in the name of 'gender identity' (synthetic sex identities) that have no medical criteria and cannot be found with any diagnostic tool. The identities exist only in the imaginations of young people captivated by a propaganda marketing apparatus of the very MIC that stands to profit from them from one end of their lives to the other.

#7

Technology, 'gender identity' and the normalization of paraphilias[7]

The conflation of paraphilias with healthy sexuality is a dangerous one, and it is a conflation that is happening under the 'gender identity' umbrella. It is posed as a human rights movement, but it is dehumanizing. This is not an accident. 'Gender identity', driven by elites invested in normalizing transsexualism and transhumanism, is part of a techno-medical complex, using the internet to spread their ideology.

The main engines normalizing paraphilias are the internet, a hatred of the natural world (biophobia) and, by extension, a hatred of women who represent the regeneration of the natural world. The internet, the beating heart of the techno dystopia we are

---

7   First published 7 July 2021, updated 15 October 2022. <https://www.the11th hourblog.com/post/technology-gender-identity-and-the-normalization-of-paraphilias>

entering, is changing our cultures, our thoughts, our world, and what it means to be human faster than we can process what is happening to us.

This apparatus is wedded to the industries that have formed around the sexual objectification of women for profit: pornography, prostitution, surrogacy, and now 'gender identity'. They are driving these industries faster than we can resist them.

The internet is not a tool that was developed so we can all hang out in one big global coffee shop and have conversations. It was an instrument used by the military for spying and is now a vehicle for driving the propaganda of the state into our homes, businesses, and into our consciousness. It is being used to control us.

The more we move away from who and what we are, organically, as parts of a living system, the more we become entrenched in technology, and the more of our lives we trade off. This process eroticizes death over life. Today, we often 'choose' sexual objectification over the desire for connection, dead machines over living entities, robots and artificial intelligence over living consciousness, and more men are gravitating to sex robots over women who are alive. We celebrate our dissociation as progressive. We have become compulsively addicted to that which does not reciprocate.

Sexuality is a word used for sexual attraction and sexual orientation toward another person, either of the same sex, the opposite sex, or both sexes. It is based on connection, interest, desire, mutuality, and embodiment.

Paraphilias are something different, usually referred to as perversions or psychosexual disorders, in which sexual gratification is obtained through practices or fantasies involving a bizarre, deviant, or highly unusual source of sexual arousal such as an animal or an object, which may prevent or hinder one's ability to reciprocate in an intimate relationship with another person.

What makes paraphilias bizarre or deviant is not some prudish resistance by most of society, but their obsessive, dissociating, compulsive and objectifying qualities as they pertain to one's erotic arousal. These elements of paraphilias are what prevent intimacy and connection with others. Sexual compulsions, like addictions, center those with paraphilias in desperation; a desperation they inflict on others because others can never satisfy the longing for connection people with paraphilias and addictions need but simultaneously repel.

The further we move away from sexual attraction based on connection with others, and based in physical embodiment, the more we insist that paraphilias should be socially normalized, as in the current 'gender identity', or anti-reality movement, which is a sexually dissociative and objectifying expression.

Sex and sexual attraction are being deconstructed for profiteering, eugenics, and social engineering, forcing our evolution away from life and melding us with machines. These experiences are being driven by technologies developing much faster than they can be harnessed. They are controlled by elites who, satiated by the things that money can buy, thrive on an ability to control others to satisfy their desperation.

Life is connection. Sex is connection. Paraphilias are addiction, obsessiveness, rumination, control and objectification – and they destroy connection. They are anti-life.

As the profiteering off women and technological developments advance, escalated by a totalitarian market that feeds off human suffering, animal torture, and the ravaging of our planet, we swerve out of control like addicts heading out into the long night. We are possessed and cannot see the forest through the trees or where all this dissociation leads.

'Gender identity', deconstructing sex by violating the boundary between male and female with surgeries and chemicals and calling this endeavor a 'treatment' for people who attempt to disown their sex, or as expression, is to invest in the complete undermining of reality. It supports and eroticizes the death spiral we are in as a species. It is the religion of those driving us into the techno dystopia we are on the brink of.

We must look deeper at what is transpiring. We must fight for and choose life. We must regard paraphilias as the addictions born of disconnection that they are if we wish to pull out of this death spiral.

#8
Martine Rothblatt:
A founding father of the
transgender empire[8]

Silver Spring MD: Martine Rothblatt, CEO of United Therapies and former CEO of SiriusXM. Photo © Andre Chung

At the heart of the emerging 'gender identity' industry is a man in a dress, donning women's breasts with the confidence only a man could acquire after a lifetime of being a first-class citizen. Martine Rothblatt, born in 1954, is an exceedingly accomplished entrepreneur and lawyer. As the founder of United Therapeutics, he was the top earning CEO in the biopharmaceutical industry. He identifies as a transsexual and transhumanist and has written extensively on the connections between the two. Rothblatt

---

8   First published 6 July 2020, *Uncommon Ground Media*. <https://uncommon groundmedia.com/martine-rothblatt-a-founding-father-of-the-transgender-empire/>

believes that human sexual dimorphism is tantamount to South African Apartheid and that transgenderism is an on-ramp to transhumanism – which is for him an exercise in overcoming 'fleshism'.

As a member of the International Conference on Transgender Law and Employment Policy (ICTLEP) since 1992, Rothblatt authored the first draft of the Transsexual and Transgender Health Law Reports, after meeting Phyllis Frye, another transgender lawyer, in Texas. This small meeting of men with a penchant for wearing women's undergarments was the launch pad for an international project to drive transsexualism globally and deconstruct human sexual dimorphism. The document Rothblatt drafted would later be referred to as the International Bill of Gender Rights (IBGR). Phyllis Frye has been referred to as the "grandmother of the transgender movement." Though Rothblatt's transhumanist preoccupations may garner him more attention, we must consider him as much of an influence in normalizing transsexualism (before it was rebranded transgenderism), as Frye, if not more.

The Conference of Transsexual and Transgender Law and Employment Policy became an international project once Frye was contacted by a transsexual identifying female in the UK named Stephen Whittle, now a professor of equalities law at Manchester Metropolitan University and president-elect of the World Professional Association for Transgender Health (WPATH) which has since developed an American branch (USPATH) as well as others: EPATH, AsiaPATH, CPATH, AusPATH and PATHA.

Whittle too has been extremely instrumental in driving trans activism, especially in the UK. She became part of the human rights experts team who elaborated on the international human rights guidelines, the Yogyakarta Principles (YP) at Gadjah Mada University in Yogyakarta, Indonesia in November 2006. In November 2017, the meeting added SOGI (Sexual Orientation Gender Identity) principles to the YP, known as plus 10. Used as international legal guidelines, they are not actually law but are being treated as such by LGBT NGOs fronting for the medical industrial complex with an investment in future medical-tech identities. The 'gender experts' are self-manufactured professionals, much like the mythology of 'gender identity' itself.

The Transsexual and Transgender Health Law Reports initiated by Frye and Rothblatt and then Whittle became a working draft for another global document and committee outlining transsexual/transgender rights in the UK, the Interdepartmental Working Group on Transsexual People, advanced by yet another male transsexual lawyer, Christine Burns, and set up by the Home Secretary of the UK in 1999. Membership of the working group included representatives from Scotland, Ireland, Wales and the US.

These four lawyers, all identifying as transsexuals, have been the main generators of a project to deconstruct sex within the law on a global scale, and to have it replaced with medical identities representing how people feel about their bodies. But Martine Rothblatt has gone much further in this deconstruction process.

The quest for trans-be-manism

Within a few years of the Conference on Transgender Law and Employment Policy (ICTLEP) driven by Rothblatt, Frye, Whittle, and Burns, Rothblatt studied for a PhD in medical ethics in London. He was granted a PhD in 2001, based on his dissertation on the conflict between private and public interest in xenotransplantation – any procedure that involves the transplantation, implantation or infusion into a human recipient of live cells, tissues, or organs from a nonhuman animal source. He later created a pig farm to harvest organs, in hopes of eventual use in humans. His purpose is to create everlasting life for humanity by continual replacement of organs as they wear out.

Rothblatt is a tenacious and accomplished individual. He's worked in Washington, D.C. in the field of communications satellite law. He has worked for NASA, was the CEO of GeoStar and the co-creator of SiriusXM Satellite Radio.

He also led the International Bar Association's biopolitical (an intersectional field between human biology and politics) project to develop a draft of Universal Declaration on the Human Genome and Human Rights for the United Nations (whose final version was adopted by the UNESCO on November 11, 1997, and endorsed by the United Nations General Assembly on December 9, 1998). He has written extensively on the need to overhaul our system of labeling people as either male or female based only on their genitalia, digital immortality and the future of creating humans, new reproductive technology, genetic screening and DNA-mapping.

Rothblatt not only believes we can live indefinitely, but after meeting Ray Kurzweil of Google and being enamored with Kurzweil's singularity theory, he created a religious organization, Terasem Movement to promote the geoethical (world ethical) use of nanotechnology for human life extension. Terasem conducts educational programs and supports scientific research and development in the areas of cryogenics, biotechnology, and cyber consciousness. Rothblatt has worked in partnership with Kurzweil promoting a screen adaptation of *The Singularity Is Near*.

Rothblatt appeared with his wife Bina, and their daughter, Jenesis, on the View in 2016 and was interviewed by Whoopi Goldberg (note of interest: Goldberg is the host of a trans reality TV modeling show). There was a fourth member of the family available for interviewing as well. Bina48 is a robot created by Rothblatt that is a replica of his wife both inside and out. It is Rothblatt's intention to install Bina's consciousness into his robot and eventually distill it to digital data to live in cyber space indefinitely. He fully believes robots are people without skin – hence he sees it as transcendence from 'fleshism'.

Rothblatt authored a peer-reviewed essay in 2008, published for the Institute of Ethics and Emerging Technologies, entitled 'Are We Transbemans Yet?' while he was still the head of United Therapeutics. The essay speculates about reinventing our species and coins a new term called beme. He wrote:

The bottom line of this essay is that in an Information Age society the 'beme is mightier than the gene'. This means that transmissible units of character or existence are more important than genetic information. For example, most people's love-mate is a person with whom they share no genetic commonality outside of that which is in the general gene pool of their community. However, a lasting interpersonal relationship is only possible if the two partners share a strong appreciation for each other's bemes – their characters, natures, and ideational units of existence.

To say the 'beme is mightier than the gene' is to disagree with the socio-cultural implication of 'blood is thicker than water'. Most people's strongest relationship, that with their spouse, or with a best friend, is not a blood relationship. On the other hand, bemes are not like mere water. A person builds up his or her bemes over time and evolves them as appears most conducive to an enjoyable life. More apropos than 'blood is thicker than water' is 'minds are deeper than matter'.

This essay aims to open our eyes to the fact that because our society is now based upon bemes more than genes it must logically re-conceptualize its species boundary.

It's been less than thirty years since Rothblatt authored that first document to create a legal fiction of disembodiment and just over ten years since he wrote about re-conceptualizing our species sex boundaries. We are now facing the normalization of that dissociation from sexed reality in the emerging industry of 'gender identity'. Shouldn't we be considering if this is what we want for ourselves? Are we ready to allow for the deconstruction of the very thing that makes us human, our biological roots in sex? Because if we are not, now is the time to act. The normalization of disembodiment has already been institutionalized and is deeply embedded in the marketplace. Children are being used in experiments both psychological and medical which are dissociating them from their bodies. Their schools have become indoctrination farms, the largest international law firm in the world has been recruited to help with the legal construction of the 'transgender child' and an estimate of more than 300 clinics have arisen in the US alone in the past ten years to manipulate their puberty and hormones, sending them down a life-long path of medicalization at a time when we have never been more set apart from each other by machines.

The jig is up on this purported 'human rights movement'. If we want to hold fast to our humanity, there is no time to waste. We are *in the eleventh hour* and must end this tech-driven, hubristic flight from flesh, mortality, and nature.

#9

The billionaires behind the LGBT movement[9]

Not long ago, the gay rights movement was a small group of people struggling to follow their dispositions within a larger heterosexual culture. Gays and lesbians were underdogs, vastly outnumbered and loosely organized, often subject to discrimination and abuse. Their story was tragic, their suffering dramatized by AIDS and Rock Hudson, *Brokeback Mountain* and Matthew Shepard.

Today's movement, however, looks nothing like that band of persecuted outcasts. The LGBT rights agenda – note the addition of 'T' – has become a powerful, aggressive force in American society. Its advocates stand at the top of media, academia, the professions, and, most important, Big Business and Big Philanthropy. Consider the following case.

Jon Stryker is the grandson of Homer Stryker, an orthopedic surgeon who founded the Stryker Corporation. Based in Kalamazoo, Michigan, the Stryker Corporation sold $13.6 billion in surgical supplies and software in 2018. (The company is now, in 2023, worth $109 billion.) Jon, the heir to the fortune, is gay. In 2000, he created the Arcus Foundation, a non-profit serving the LGBT community, because of his own experience coming out as homosexual. Arcus has given more than $58.4 million to programs and organizations doing LGBT-related work between 2007 and 2010 alone, making it one of the largest LGBT funders in the world. Stryker gave more than $30 million to Arcus himself in that three-year period, through his stock in Stryker Medical Corporation.

Stryker founded Arcus right when the AIDS epidemic was being brought under control in the US. Before he started Arcus, he

9   First published 21 January 2020, *First Things*. <https://www.firstthings.com/web-exclusives/2020/01/the-billionaires-behind-the-lgbt-movement>

was president of Depot Landmark LLC, a development company specializing in rehabilitating historical buildings. This would serve him well when he later renovated space for Arcus in Kalamazoo. He was also a founding board member of Greenleaf Trust, a privately held wealth management firm also based in Kalamazoo.

Jon's sister Ronda Stryker is married to William Johnston, chairman of Greenleaf Trust. She is also vice chair of Spelman College, on which Arcus recently bestowed a $2 million grant in the name of lesbian feminist Audre Lorde. The money is earmarked for a queer studies program. Ronda and Johnston have gifted Spelman $30 million overall, the largest gift from living donors in its 137-year history. She is also a trustee of Kalamazoo College (on which Arcus bestowed a social justice leadership grant for $23 million in 2012), as well as a member of the Harvard Medical School Board of Fellows.

Pat Stryker, another sister to Jon, has worked closely with gay male Tim Gill. Gill operates one of the largest LGBT non-profits in America and has been close to the Stryker family since Jon created Arcus. In 1999, Tim Gill sold his stakes to Quark, his computer software company, and began running the Gill Foundation in Colorado. Working closely with Pat Stryker and two other wealthy philanthropists – who together became known as the four horsemen due to their ruthless political strategies – they set out to change Colorado, a red state, to blue. They proceeded to pour half a billion dollars into small groups advocating LGBT agendas. Gill noted in his opening introduction of Jon Stryker at the 2015 GLSEN Respect Awards that, since knowing each other, he and Jon have "plotted, schemed, hiked and skied together," while also "punishing the wicked and rewarding the good."

Prior to 2015, Stryker had already built the political infra-structure to drive gender identity ideology and transgenderism across the globe, donating millions to small and large entities. These included hundreds of thousands of dollars to ILGA, an LGBT organization for equality in Europe and Central Asia with 54 countries participating, and Transgender Europe, a voice for the trans community in Europe and Asia with 43 countries participating (Transgender Europe has also funded smaller organizations like TENI, Transgender Equality Network Ireland).

In 2008, Arcus founded the Arcus Operating Foundation, an arm of the foundation that organizes conferences, leadership programs, and research publications. At one 2008 meeting in Bellagio, Italy, 29 international leaders committed to expanding global philanthropy to support LGBT rights. At the meeting, along with Stryker and Ise Bosch, founder of Dreilinden Fund in Germany, was Michael O'Flaherty – one of the rapporteurs for the Yogyakarta Principles on the Application of International Human Rights Law in Relation to Sexual Orientation and Gender Identity (principles outlined in Indonesia in 2006). With the Yogyakarta Principles, the seeds were planted to bring in and attach gender identity ideology to our legal structures. O'Flaherty has been an elected member of the United Nations Human Rights Committee since 2004.

Out of the Bellagio meeting Arcus created MAP, the LGBT Movement Advancement Project, to track the complex system of advocacy and funding that would promote gender identity/transgenderism in the culture. Simultaneously, the LGBTI Core Group was formed as an informal cross-regional group of United Nations member countries to represent LGBTI human rights issues to the UN. Core Group members funded by Arcus include Outright Action International and The American Human Rights Campaign. Core Group member countries include Albania, Australia, Brazil, Chile, Colombia, Costa Rica, Croatia, El Salvador, France, Germany, Israel, Italy, Japan, Montenegro, Mexico, New Zealand, Norway, Spain, the United Kingdom, the United States, Uruguay, and the European Union, as well as the Office of the UN High Commissioner for Human Rights.

These groups all promote gender identity and transgenderism by training leaders in political activism, leadership, transgender law, religious liberty, education, and civil rights. The line-up of Arcus-supported organizations advancing the cause is daunting:

Victory Institute, the Center for American Progress, the ACLU, the Transgender Law Center, Trans Justice Funding Project, OutRight Action International, Human Rights Watch, GATE, Parliamentarians for Global Action (PGA), The Council for Global Equality, the United Nations, Amnesty International, and GLSEN. The Sexuality Information and Education Council of the US (SIECUS), in partnership with Advocates for Youth, Answer, GLSEN, the Human Rights Campaign (HRC) Foundation, and Planned Parenthood Federation of America (PPFA), has initiated a campaign using a rights-based framework to inform approaches in reshaping cultural narratives of sexuality and reproductive health. Sixty-one additional organizations have signed a letter supporting an overhaul of current curriculums.

US Secretary of State, John Kerry, introduces financier and philanthropist George Soros who spoke with Assistant Secretary for Public Affairs Doug Frantz about strengthening civil society, democracy, and the world economy at the US Department of State's Open Forum in Washington, D.C., on 13 May 2014. (State Department photo, Public Domain)

In 2013, Adrian Coman, a veteran of George Soros's Open Society Foundations (a driver of transgender ideology that has begun initiatives to normalize transgender children), was named director of the international human rights program at the Arcus Foundation to drive gender identity ideology globally. Previously, Coman served as program director of the International Gay and Lesbian Human Rights Commission. And in 2015, Arcus worked closely with and funded NoVo Foundation programs for transgenderism. NoVo was founded by Peter Buffett, son of billionaire Warren Buffett.

These programs and initiatives advance gender identity ideology by supporting various faith organizations, sports and cultural associations, police department training, and educational programs in grade schools and high schools (GLSEN – whose founder was brought to Arcus in 2012 on the board of directors – has influenced many K-12 school curricula), and universities and medical institutions – including the American Psychological Foundation (APF). Arcus funds help APF (the leading psychology organization in the United States) develop guidelines for establishing trans-affirmative psychological practices. Psychologists are 'encouraged' by those monies to modify their understanding of gender, broadening the range of biological reality to include abstract, medical identities.

Concurrently, Arcus drives gender identity ideology and transgenderism in the marketplace by encouraging businesses to invest in LGBT causes. Lest we forget, Stryker is heir to a $133.55 billion (figure updated in April 2024) medical corporation. One only has to look at the corporations supporting LGBT during Pride Month each year to ascertain the success Arcus has had in this arena.

As the example of the Arcus Foundation shows, the LGB civil rights movement of yore has morphed into a relentless behemoth, one that has strong ties to the medical industrial complex and global corporatists. The pharmaceutical lobby is the largest lobbying entity in Congress. Although activists present the LGBT movement as a weak, powerless group suffering oppression and discrimination, in truth, it wields enormous power and influence – power it increasingly uses to remake our laws, schools, and society.

#10

Astraea: Arcus Foundation's lesbian front for the gender industry, the erasure of women and the colonization of human sex in the global south[10]

In 1977, a group of ten New York City women started a small philanthropic organization to support the work of lesbians and women of color. They came from a variety of backgrounds.

Shortly thereafter, the organization now known as Astraea Lesbian Foundation for Justice was born. Reporting on its history for *Them* magazine in 2019, Elyssa Goodman spoke with its former director, who said, "initially no one wanted to fund them because they were an organization focused on the needs of lesbians and people of color." The women were from various classes and ethnicities and decided to create a program that would primarily award funding to other groups led by lesbians and women of color. The funded organizations ran the gamut from gay liberation, workers' rights, anti-war initiatives, civil rights, environmental principles, and more. The founding mothers of Astraea created one of the world's first funds entirely for women. They decreed Astraea would always be comprised of at least 50% women of color.

In 1980, Goodman reported, the organization's first grants were given to women organizers and artists throughout the Northeastern United States and ranged from $100 to $1,000. The grants went to supporting the rights of incarcerated women, helping lesbian mothers maintain child custody, the development of women's

---

10 First published 28 June 2021, updated 15 October 2022. <https://www.the11thhourblog.com/post/astraea-arcus-foundation-s-front-for-the-gender-industry-the-erasure-of-lesbians>

art spaces, and even a lesbian choir. Astraea became a national organization in 1990.

The first winners of Astraea's Lesbian Writers Fund, started in 1991, were: Melinda Goodman, Yasmin V. Tambiah, Mariana Romo-Carmona, Magdalena Zscokke and Ana Maria Simo, judged by Audre Lorde, Jewelle Gomez, Gloria Anzaldua, and Sarah Schulman. That year, the organization also bestowed its Sappho Award of Distinction and grant upon Audre Lorde.

Those were the days. Women for women. I could weep with feelings of nostalgia.

A few years later the men moved into LGB social justice work and brought in all the earmarks of big business. The Gill Foundation was founded in 1994 and began driving vast sums of money to create systematic change with big donors and eventually the power of big money. It represented, for Gill Foundation founder, Tim Gill, a huge metamorphosis in philanthropy, which reflected changes in the economy. The so-called "new economy," according to Gill

> which had its roots in the high-technology industry, resulted in more people with disposable income than ever before. Moreover, many of the new economy donors brought with them the values and business practices they had learned from the for-profit community, combined with a desire to create social change in the same way their risk-taking helped create the new economy.

Once gay marriage was procured in the US, in 2015, Gill was thinking just like the businessman he is. Gender identity became the new cause célèbre for his LGBT non-governmental organization (NGO). Gender identity opened markets in sexual identity, identities needing protection. By 2018, 'transgender' and 'gender identity' took center stage on their funding report.

In 2000, Jon Stryker, banker and heir to a multi-billion dollar medical corporation, founded the LGBT NGO Arcus Foundation, which was to see the deconstruction of lesbian culture, the rise of fetishism, and the gender identity market where lesbians, gays, and bisexuals who were once offered support in a grassroots movement of their kin are now being erased.

In 2007, Astraea Foundation received its first Arcus Foundation grant and its focus began to shift from women to sexual and 'gender minorities'. Over the years, Astraea Foundation has seen close to twelve million dollars in funding from Arcus Foundation, the most donations to any of Arcus Foundation grantees. By 2020, all that was left of lesbians on the Astraea Foundation welcome page was the L in the LGBTQI+ acronym.

In 2010, the grants to Astraea took another slight shift to supporting 'gender minorities' specifically in the global south, a distinct focus of Arcus Foundation. In 2011, beyond their usual hundreds of thousands in annual funding from Arcus, they received $200,000, specifically for initiating the Global Action for Trans Equality (GATE), a gender industry organization fighting for the depathologization of body dissociation and the erosion of women's sex-based rights and sexual orientation. By 2012, Astraea was receiving three separate grants in the hundreds of thousands from Arcus Foundation.

In 2013, GATE got together in Berlin with other gender industry activists and funders to explore new ways to bring resources to 'trans' communities. At a subsequent meeting two years later in Istanbul, the International Trans Fund (ITF) was born, to drive gender identity ideology south. Funded with two and half million dollars from Arcus Foundation to create the initiative, Astraea Lesbian Foundation, also supported by Open Society Foundations and the US government under the Obama administration, hosted the meeting.

In 2013, Astraea Foundation, among other monies that they received from Arcus Foundation, also procured $50,000 for the Global Philanthropy Project (GPP). GPP is the primary thought-leader and go-to partner for donor coordination on global LGBTI work. GPP Director, Mathew Hart, together with the Astraea Foundation, has coordinated a movement to discredit those resisting gender identity ideology, framing anyone who disagrees with this ideology of body dissociation, as rabid, bigoted, and religious conservatives, setting the international stage for global online conferences to promote the same. This GPP and Astraea Foundation movement to discredit those who critique gender ideology, is driven by the Arcus Foundation and is partnered with The Baring Foundation in the UK, Dreilinden GmbH in Germany, and ironically, The Global Fund for Women.

In 2014, the 'I' was added to the LGBTQ+ matrix to support the idea that there is a multiplicity of sexes (a new marketing constituency buying medical identities).

By 2017, China, Dominican Republic, Haiti, India, Jamaica, Trinidad and Tobago were added to the countries being colonized by Arcus Foundation, through deep funding to Astraea, to drive gender identity ideology (body dissociation) through the global south. A grant to Astraea to buttress the idea that intersex constitutes other human sexes received a whopping $400,000 grant.

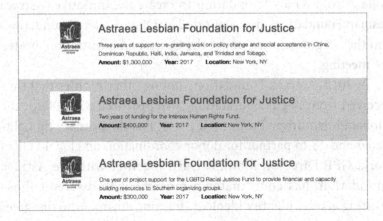

China opened its first gender clinic for children in 2021.

By 2018, the Astraea Foundation was in full post-modernist mode, supporting queer identities and celebrating their part in getting gender bills passed.

What has all this activism and money from the good ol' boys network culminated in? In funding for men of course, with a mission to empower 'trans women'. In 2020, the Astraea Foundation now exists as a handmaiden of the Arcus Foundation, Stryker Medical, and the global movement toward dissociation from sexed reality for the profiteering of the medical industrial complex. Astraea also receives funding from the AbbVie Foundation, part of the global pharma giant that makes the puberty blocker, Lupron, playing a starring role in the arrested development of children caught up in the gender industry. Through its lesbian front for Arcus Foundation, its funding supports the conversion therapy of young lesbians in the guise of gender identity and the male fetishization of womanhood, with an ultimate social engineering goal of deconstructing human sexual dimorphism and the erasure or women. Astraea Lesbian Foundation Mission and Vision statements now advocate for everyone's issues, aside it seems, lesbians, who have been erased.

#11

The ACLU drives legal precedents for dissociation from sexed reality[11]

A once legal bastion in high regard on both sides of the political spectrum, with a commitment to defending Americans' constitutional rights, the American Civil Liberties Union (ACLU), has become a weapon of the state, a defender of the gender industry fronting for the techno-medical complex (TMC) and transhumanist ideology. It upholds that human sexual dimorphism is not real and is raking in funding from America's monied elites to defend this lie.

A current legal case fought by the ACLU against the state of Arkansas utilized a $15-million endowment from Jon Stryker, heir to the Stryker Medical Corporation fortune worth $133.55 billion (2024), and his husband, Slobodan Randjelović, to secure a win. The gift was to assist in overturning a state ban that refused to allow for drug and surgical experimentation on children's reproductive organs.

The gift from Stryker and Randjelović is one of several large endowments from philanthropic elites, deeply invested in the TMC and invested in institutionalizing gender ideology. This includes Arcus Foundation funding. The Arcus Foundation is the most significant LGBT non-governmental organization in the world. It has helped build the political infrastructure to drive dissociation from sexed reality as a human right. It was founded by Jon Stryker and he uses the money from stock in his medical empire to fund it. Dissociation from sexed reality framed as a human right is part

11   First published 23 July 2023. <https://jbilek.substack.com/p/the-aclu-drives-legal-precedents?utm_source=%2Fsearch%2FThe%2520ACLU%2520Drives&utm_medium=reader2>

of a transhumanist paradigm which promotes a reality beyond our current human borders that are anchored in sex.

In a press release in January 2022, the ACLU announced that its historic docket of Supreme Court cases will be named after Joan and Irwin Jacobs, two longtime ACLU supporters whose estimated worth in 2017 was $1.23 billion. The Supreme Court Docket naming is made possible through the Jacobs' landmark $20 million gifts to the ACLU Foundation's Bill of Rights endowment fund – the largest endowment gift in the ACLU's history.

In 1968, alongside Leonard Kleinrock and Andrew Viterbi, Irwin Jacobs co-founded Linkabit Corporation, a San Diego-based technology company. They later co-founded Qualcomm, a multinational visionary telecommunication giant with over 30,000 employees in all corners of the globe, as well as one of today's innovation leaders. Jacobs has donated hundreds of millions of dollars to several educational institutions, organizations and schools focused on the fields of engineering, computer science, and communications.

Together the Jacobs have funded the Center on Global Transformation, providing a new framework for exploration and analysis shaping the forces of economic change in the world at the University of California San Diego (UCSD), where they also have an engineering school in their name. They donated $110 million to the engineering program in 2003 with departments in nanoengineering, bioengineering and AI. They provided a $75 million lead gift for a new facility at UCSD Health Center in 2010; then a 'challenge gift' brought their contributions to a total of $100 million. The center was named for them and helped UCSD Health become a leader listed in the LGBT Human Rights Campaign Healthcare Equality Index in 2018. UCSD Health offers, not inconsequentially, 'gender affirming care'.

In December 2021, UCSD Medical School hosted a 'transgender healthcare' symposium to provide a comprehensive review of different aspects of 'gender affirming medical care'. This event featured sessions on 'gender-sensitive cultural awareness', behavioral health care, primary care, and 'medical and surgical gender affirming interventions'.

Upon completion of the symposium, it was anticipated that participants would be able to:

- Identify appropriate terminology and pronouns for 'gender identity' and sexual orientation including gender-neutral pronouns.
- Summarize 'gender affirmation' surgeries and appropriate referrals.
- Discuss 'gender affirming' surgeries available at UC San Diego Health.
- Discuss options for fertility preservation in 'transgender and non-binary' individuals.
- Identify key mental health issues in the 'transgender/non-binary' community.
- Describe the requirements needed for mental health providers to provide support for 'gender affirming' surgeries.
- Describe healthcare issues related to 'transgender and non-binary' adolescents and young adults.
- Identify how to improve the patient experience for 'transgender/non-binary' patients for better overall healthcare outcomes.

The Jacobs also donated $133 million to create the Joan and Irwin Jacobs Technion-Cornell Institute, a global technology institute with a presence on three continents, including China. The institute hosted a transgender symposium during the 17th Annual Seminar on Patient-Physician Relations. Cornell University, with which Technion is partnered, has published a Transgender Guide to 'Transitioning' and 'Gender Affirmation' in the Workplace.

The Jacobs provided the most significant gift ever to be bestowed on the Salk Institute (SI) for $100 million, which would help raise an additional $200 million for SI. The SI is embracing the artificial intelligence revolution and inventing new ways to investigate life. SI, with its DEI program, also supports the gender industry and gender identity ideology which refutes the reality of sexual dimorphism in humans.

Joan and Irwin Jacobs also spent millions of dollars getting their granddaughter elected to congress in 2020, who is now stumping for the gender industry, a subsidiary of the techno-medical complex. Congresswoman Sara Jacobs represented California's 53rd Congressional District and outperformed her opponent with more significant experience. The figures on Jacobs' three years of tax returns, when they finally emerged before the election, also undoubtedly played a role in her outpacing Georgette Gomez, her rival and then the San Diego City Council president. Gomez paid nearly $9,000 in taxes on $82,000 income in 2019, while Jacobs' 2019 taxes were reported at $1.46 million on an income of $7.19 million.

Settling right into her role as a shill for the techno-medical complex, Jacobs rolled out her pitch for LGBT, using the now tired and worn tactic of sewing a made-up ideology promoting dissociation from our sexed reality to the LGB human rights movement and hitting all the high notes. These included bogus statistics to cultivate sympathy, including suicide and bullying, a need for training teachers about the bullying of gender non-conforming children, homelessness, etc. Jacobs went the extra mile though and stated she had both a 'transgender' and gender non-conforming sibling. Even though the term 'transgender' had only entered the cultural lexicon two minutes ago and no one can tell us what this word means with any clarity, this didn't stop Jacobs from rolling right along as if this ideology was already engraved in stone and the term completely understood and agreed upon.

Finishing strongly in her pitch, Jacobs manipulated her audience by sharing her "firsthand experience with the hurt and pain that can be caused by misgendering someone, and how easy it is to be an ally by taking the extra time to normalize sharing your pronouns." She explained this is why she supports ensuring that it is easy to access federal identity documents with the pronouns one identifies with, and why she is using her platform to educate people about correct pronoun usage. In December 2021, she gave an impassioned plea against an epidemic of violence being experienced by 'transgender people', on the House floor. Though there is absolutely no coherent explanation of what this term means, Jacobs, like many politicians before her, performed what seemed like a faux soliloquy to drive her agenda of the political and social normalizing of synthetic sex identities.

I am experiencing déjà vu, having written about two other billionaire families, the Pritzkers and Rothblatts, each with a member of their family claiming to be the opposite sex, and their heavy investments in medical supplies, biotech, pharma, and AI.

While the gender industry is framed as human rights, what we see manifesting behind the scenes, over and over, with the most significant funders and drivers of the ideology, are enormous investments in technology, medical supplies, pharma, finance, AI, and an investment in the lie that humans can change sex. This lie is also supported by the ACLU.

#12

Techno-Capitalism, transgenderism and the colonization of female biology[12]

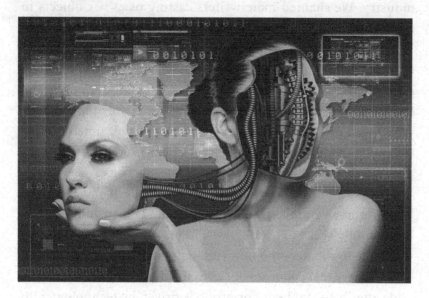

Under Techno-Capitalism, hatred of women is promoted to commodify female bodies and profit from women's pain.

Most people probably think more about the liberating elements of technology than how it drives our servitude. We may think about the drawbacks of individual technological developments, but overall, we're not thinking a lot about the unfettered growth of technology, its speed, complexity and its vast spread. As technology is sewn to unfettered capitalism it must grow or die. It must breach new boundaries or wither. Techno-Capitalism, or technology as it is wedded to capitalism, functions of its own accord now, driven by

---

12   First published 8 May 2020, *Uncommon Ground Media*. <https://uncommon groundmedia.com/techno-capitalism/>

profit. The oppression and hatred of females has become part of this system, which continually magnifies it.

In the 1960s and 70s, during the resurgence of a strong Women's Liberation Movement, women had a fighting chance to beat back against the systematized hatred of women. We rallied for physical autonomy, against rape, against the pornography industry. We shamed male writers casting us as sex objects in their novels and we had widespread media coverage of our views. We fought for equal pay for equal work. We dissected rigid sex stereotypes that subsequently successfully assimilated women and girls into the social fabric, into universities and the sciences, and into professional sports and politics. But our oppression has been repackaged by a capitalist system, driven by almost unfathomable technological developments and is now being sold back to women as empowerment, liberation, and consumerist choice.

The porn industry is worth billions annually. It endangers the lives of women and the psychological health of men and children. It constantly seeks to create new and bizarre forms of titillation with women's bodies (and now children's) standing as the detritus. This industry that colonizes our objectified bodies and tosses them aside after abusing them, for profit, is driven by technology into every sphere of our cultures. This objectification of women's biology – objectification entails hatred to sustain itself – is attached to the global market with technology driving it at warp speed. Men buy and ingest this hatred and young boys learn from it. They grow up feeling entitled to use women as objects because it is all around them, in the air they breathe. Young girls learn this hatred of themselves and play out all manner of psycho-social disorders to inflict pain on their sexed bodies. They cut their skin and starve themselves, which is seen as an aberration, a mental disease. Yet, when they graduate to selling their bodies for sex to pay college tuition and/or to stay alive, selling their eggs for profit, selling their wombs as vessels for purchased babies, to feed their families and cut off their breasts so they can identify as men, these self-inflicted wounds, under the great god of techno-capitalism, become progressive.

This body hatred is normalized by the media, controlled by the same corporations profiting from women's misery, to the point it is no longer even understood as hatred. This hatred driven by techno-capitalism looks like choice, even as it crawls across the globe, right under our noses, decimating women's and girls' lives. It looks like medical 'help' when rich, white people can purchase a woman's womb on the other side of the world so she can feed her family. The medical industrial complex (MIC) makes sure of the mother's erasure in language and law: 'surrogate' while male sperm donors keep their parentage (read: humanity): fathers.

As girls seek to have their healthy breasts removed in order to 'identify' as men, or men buy women's body 'parts' to 'identify' as females, the world celebrates their bravery. The MIC supports this, buying the complicity of institutions to support the bravery narrative and driving that narrative into the global marketplace. This creates a new 'gender identity' industry. The tech-controlled media, unrelenting in its message, drives the narrative into all our lives.

Women's bodies are a frontier to colonize.

An anonymous journalist, @DrEm (on Twitter), writing for *Uncommon Ground Media*, has coined a term for the concept of 'gender dysphoria' that young women are suddenly experiencing in vast numbers across the western world. She thinks a more apt term, and I agree with her, is 'Oppression Discomfort Disorder'. It clarifies what is really happening to young women. It takes the onus off individual women and puts it squarely back where it belongs, on society, specifically techno-capitalism. It externalizes the hatred that women continually internalize. In 2020, @DrEm published a two-part article about the sexist roots of transgenderism and how it has evolved. I have written over the years how this mythology has been organized by the MIC to drive surgeries, sales of pharmaceuticals, body dissociation as progressive, and how this is opening markets.

What we are witnessing, still, is the violation of female boundaries driven by techno-capitalism for the profit of men, sexually, mentally, materially and financially. This violation is being repackaged as progressive and sped up by techno-capitalism.

As the MIC seeks to conquer the as-yet impossible task of transplanting (dead) women's wombs into men, it is time we take a stark look at how these systems, all these industries, are linked by the techno-capitalist colonization of female biology for profit and who exactly is profiting.

#13

Is humanity ready for LGBTQ+ tech babies and the full erasure of women from reproduction?[13]

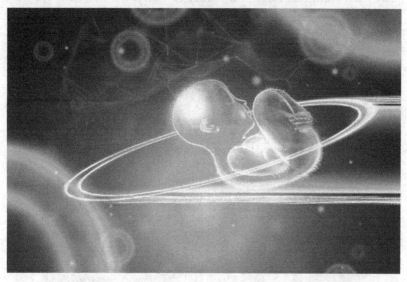

Image from Hashem Al-Ghaili's EctoLife: The World's First Artificial Womb Facility

Most liberals fighting for gay rights since the sexual revolution, myself included, had no idea of the Pandora's box they were opening.

Some elite and powerful gay men today, no longer the social outcasts they were in the 1950s, are spearheading a movement, along with rich transsexual men, to create babies from scratch. Ostracized for their sexual proclivities in the 50s and beyond, gay men wanted more than anything to be equal participants in the social fabric that heterosexual men possessed. But it was not

---

13 First published 11 June 2023, *Human Events*. <https://humanevents.com/2023/06/11/jennifer-bilek-is-humanity-ready-for-lgbtq-tech-babies-and-the-full-erasure-of-women-from-reproduction>

enough to secure the right to gay partnerships with the legal parity of heterosexuals, and to take part as equal members of society, as liberals understood their fight.

Gay male philanthropist, David C. Bohnett, chairman of the David Bohnett Foundation, articulated the thrust we now see coming from the LGBT Inc. corporate coalition perfectly: "Gay men want marriage and family equality."

The only way for gay men to have family equality with heterosexuals is to generate the ability to have their own biological children within the institution of marriage. Gay marriage has already been secured within the US, and the powerful LGBT non-governmental organizations (NGOs) that came up to secure it are now set upon deconstructing sexual dimorphism which we see taking place in many societies with the introduction of gender ideology, under the banner of new LGBT human rights.

LGBT NGOs and the rich gay and transsexual philanthropist men funding them, are rearranging the organization of society around our species' dimorphic sex. Women are being erased in language and law, and an usurpation of our reproduction capacities is well under way.

With Tim Gill and Jon Stryker, and their mammoth LGBT (initially LGB) NGOs, the Gill Foundation and the Arcus Foundation, pouring billions of dollars into spreading an ideology of disembodiment, gay men who dream of sexual parity with heterosexual men are on the cusp of having their dreams realized. In California, a new bill aiming for 'fertility equity' would ensure funding for gay male couples to buy women, implant embryos in their wombs, and then take the babies away at the point of birth.

Transsexual men who fetishize womanhood and attempt to own it through medical technology, once at the very fringe of sexual-identities-gone-corporate, have suddenly become very convenient, and have taken center stage in the LGBT agenda to deconstruct sex.

Other rich and powerful gay male philanthropists – Mark S. Bonham, with a queer sexuality center in Canada, and the now deceased Ric Weiland, the second person to be employed at Microsoft – have helped create a political juggernaut of what is now a ridiculously long acronym representing powerful corporate interests. Men with a fetish of owning female biology, such as Martine Rothblatt, a transsexual transhumanist lawyer and entrepreneur who authored the first 'gender bill', writes and speaks often about 'transgenderism' fertilizing the ground for transhumanism. He also has a penchant for AI and now sits on the board of the Mayo Clinic.

Petra De Sutter, a politician and Professor of gynecology at Ghent University – and since 2020 a Deputy Prime Minister of Belgium – has given talks about the future of technological reproduction, sans women. Assistant Health Secretary of the US, Rachel Levine, and Jennifer Pritzker, men who have appropriated female biology through surgery, have helped engineer a corporate coup to usurp female reproduction under the guise of a human right to express oneself by surgically altering one's sex characteristics. Along with this engineering of human reproduction comes the changing of what we understand ourselves to be, a sexually dimorphic species. We are on a trajectory toward post-humanism.

With the advent of CRISPR/Cas9 gene editing, medical technology is growing exponentially. Gay men and men who fetishize being women are on the verge of finally taking their place amongst the other men, vying for the right to control women's bodies and procreative capacities.

While most of society is still reeling from the shock that men are being allowed into women's safe spaces and sports, and who are equally as fascinated with people who've appropriated the physical characteristics of the opposite sex, they remain in the dark about what is happening under pretense of human rights.

Activists in Italy (FINAARGIT), recently protesting the advances of technological reproduction and transhumanism, are far more aware of the gender industry and its threat. North Americans, ensconced in the media echo chamber created by Big Pharma and Big Tech propaganda, are still caught up in the corporate hype about a marginalized group of people with body dysmorphia needing society to be overhauled so they can feel safe.

The political right in the US screams that the political left has engineered the destructive gender industry, putting women and children at risk. They have set themselves up as lone saviors, while ignoring decades of work by feminists to root out this industry and its assault on women. The political left screams that the political right wants to control women's bodies and reproductive rights with abortion laws. The right and the left are both correct: they both want control of women's reproductive capacities.

The Democratic Party drives the narrative that men can be women (possess their biology through technology) while investing in the tech reproductive market, such as Jeff Bezos, who launched Amazon's first fertility platform in 2019. Vast profits will be generated from the sterilization of children who have succumbed to a corporate propaganda campaign telling them they can switch their sex. The Republicans, on the other hand, are hellbent on monitoring women's choice to gestate through control of reproduction laws, while throwing money at companies to monitor their cycles, such as 28 femtech, the investment choice of gay conservative billionaire, Peter Thiel. Then there is Marc Benioff, multi-billionaire owner and co-founder of Salesforce Cloud Computing, and *TIME* magazine.

Neither gay nor transsexual, Benioff invests in so-called 'gender clinics' that sterilize children, and the assisted fertility market. He claims to be neither Democrat nor Republican and gave $1.5 million to both parties in 2019. The market is driving exponential advancements in medical technology to give all these power-mad men exactly what they want: access to the source of life that, so far, only women possess.

Gay marriage was the linchpin for the political apparatus we see now, tying together reproductive technology, the building of a consumer base for that technology, and the adding of the 'T' to LGB, to open markets in sexual identity and attempt to break the boundary between male and female.

The creation of synthetic facsimiles of sex, and laws that deconstruct sexual dimorphism in the guise of supporting margin-alized people, was political genius for marketing the dissolution of human sexual reproduction. At this point, the alphabet acronym is just support for the main objective: a med-tech usurping of women's fertility. LGB signals human rights. The supporting characters, T+, in the gender brigade work to obscure the industry and technology behind the façade of human rights, moving at warp speed.

Matt Krisiloff is another gay man who is investing in the biotechnology that he hopes will give him the power of creation. A young man from California's technology scene began popping up in the world's leading developmental biology labs a few years ago. These labs were deciphering the secrets of embryos and had a particular interest in how eggs are formed. Some thought if they could replicate the process of egg formation, they would be able to copy it and transmute any cell into an egg, as reported by *MIT Technology Review* in 2021.

More recently, *The New Yorker* reported on Krisiloff and the work of Japanese reproductive biologists, Katsuhiko Hayashi and Mitinori Saitou, who inspired Krisiloff's company, Conception, in Berkeley, California. The Japanese biologists are the researchers who converted the skin cells of mice into fertile eggs, outside the body. Conception was founded in 2018 and has since raised almost $40 million in venture capital to pursue in-vitro gametogenesis (IVG), an experimental technique that allows scientists to grow embryos in a lab by reprogramming adult cells to become sperm and egg cells.

The New Yorker reports that in recent years, the science of extending female reproductive longevity has seen increased interest, and biotech companies are attempting to begin clinical trials of several therapies, including new IVF techniques and pharmaceuticals, anticipating an eventual human population plateau that could affect global economies, the provision of healthcare, and the funding of pension systems.

This is happening at a time when womb transplants into men are being researched, and international breastfeeding organizations are promoting men who lactate, through technology. Media promotion of 'Throuples', a polyamorous relationship between people who claim an equal and exclusive commitment with each other, and sexual dimorphism being deconstructed in language and law in various countries via gender ideology, can only hint at the chaos brewing via these new technologies and the laws being created to support them.

Krisiloff's start up, Conception, is trying to remove the age limits on motherhood by converting blood cells into human eggs. However, his motivation runs much deeper than innovation and helping women extend the time their reproductive capacities will be successful. Krisiloff's interest in IVG is also personal, as reported by *The New Yorker*. He is gay and likes the thought of one day being able to have his biological children with a male partner.

For wealthy gay and transsexual men at the heads of finance and the techno-medical complex, deconstructing sexual dimorphism is a page taken out of Martine Rothblatt's book on genetic engineering. In Chapter Five of *Unzipped Genes* (1997), titled 'Transgenic Creationism: My Perfect Monster', Rothblatt discusses transgenics and the potential of creating designer babies, merging portions of genes from different persons or species. Rothblatt also owns a xenotransplantation farm.

Xenotransplantation is any procedure that involves the transplantation, implantation, or infusion into a human recipient of either live cells, tissues, or organs from a nonhuman animal source.

"With xenotransplantation technology," Rothblatt writes, "children have more than two immediate parents – immediate sources of genetic material – and one or more of these parents might not even be human" (*Unzipped Genes*, p. 72). These modern families are paving the way for a total colonization of human reproduction which is why the current family model is being attacked along with reproductive sex. LGBT Inc.'s tech offspring emerging from these experiments will not be rooted in a set of parental genes but in a factory compilation of genes and bodies involved in their gestation.

The 'diverse and inclusive' queer veneer these elite men are putting on a eugenics project that obliterates women as the source of life is the same old dance of woman hatred we've been dealing with for eons. But now it is amped up by a tech frenzy wedded to unfettered corporatism and the power of what has become LGBT Inc., a juggernaut of force manifested out of corporatizing sexual attraction and fetishes.

#14

Humanity for sale: The gender industry is corporate grooming for transhumanism[14]

If we understand the mechanism and motives of the group mind, it is now possible to control and regiment the masses according to our will without them knowing it.

—Edward L. Bernays

Transgender is not a type of person. It is the conglomerate name for an array of corporate pressures which groom children and adults for industrial body dissociation, thus opening humanity to further corporate encroachments into our bodies. It is the colonization of humans, directly targeting the next generation. It is, as renowned transhumanist Martine Rothblatt states, "the on-ramp to transhumanism."

The word *transgenderism* is not fit for communication. It does not define anything clearly, but rather obscures the industry manifested in its name. It's an umbrella term with no borders under which sit too many conflicting ideas, allowing its definitional goalposts to move whenever anyone critiques its ideology and the markets formed around it. Instituting gender identity as a legal concept deconstructs what it means to be human, since we are a biologically and sexually dimorphic species. What is happening is that the corporate state is deconstructing sex as a step toward alienating us from our humanity. Endless discussions about 'gender identity' obscure this fact.

For a decade, a progressive-coded language of body dissociation has taken shape simultaneously on the landscape of multiple

---

14 First published 2 March 2023, *The American Mind*. <https://americanmind.org/features/soul-dysphoria/humanity-for-sale/>

western civilizations. Terms such as gender identity, transitioning, body dysphoria, pregnant men, cervix havers, gender binary, and sexual 'spectra' of various kinds have been relentlessly regurgitated in the mainstream media. These terms, used repeatedly, dissociate individuals from their sexed realities. They are now embedded into our legal structures under the framework of human rights.

When we view humanity and our sexed realities as another frontier to open markets for corporate profiteering, what is referred to as a 'human rights movement' for people who disown their sex begins to take another shape.

Trans pays

Inclusivity is more than a social cause. It's a business opportunity. It's time to maximize your business growth.

—DMI Consulting

Body dissociation as a progressive and liberating identity is marketed to children by activist organizations, corporations, Hollywood, the music, fashion, and beauty industries, by the medical establishment, on social media, and in schools. The power of the message that dissociating from one's sexed body is progressive comes from its relentless saturation throughout the mainstream media, an oligopoly that constructs a hegemonic narrative and many of whose outlets are supported by BlackRock and Vanguard, two American multinational investment companies with trillions of dollars in assets and a concerted interest in this narrative.

Authentic Brands Group received an $875 million investment from BlackRock in 2019. Authentic Brands Group owns 50 brands, including *Sports Illustrated*, which has now featured two men posing as women on its covers.

Its Aeropostale brand donates money to LGBT causes from its 'gender-neutral' collection.

Vanguard was the largest shareholder of Marqeta Inc., a global credit card-issuing platform. Visa, with Marqeta Inc., supported

Daylight, a new 'queer credit card' and digital banking platform established in 2020, that folded in 2023 after raising $20 million in funding. Daylight marketed its card to sell assisted medical tech fertility procedures to the lesbian and gay community and to those children who are now offered the invitation to purchase synthetic sexes (the T and Q in LGBTQ+) at the cost of their future fertility. It was the first LGBTQ+ financial technology, or fintech, banking platform. It also provided a credit score for businesses by their adherence to LGBT-established protocols.

Global Market Insights projects a compound annual growth rate of 11.5% between 2023 and 2032 for surgeries to create synthetic sex characteristics. This growth rate does not include growing trends in clavicle-shortening surgeries, operations on men's feet to make them appear smaller, or the complications created by these unnecessary operations to attack and rearrange the sex and other characteristics of healthy young bodies to help men appear as the opposite sex, as eunuchs, or as both sexes. This market analysis doesn't include the dangerous drugs used on young people, such as puberty blockers and cross-sex hormones. Increased sales of anesthesia, antibiotics, and anti-rejection medications for creating synthetic sex body parts used to socially obscure natal sex is also not accounted for in the projected growth market. Medical supplies, research, clinics, and special training for new and complex surgeries are not tallied in the projected profits.

The great rebrand

The word *transgenderism* is a rebranding of the word *transsexualism*, which is rooted in transvestic fetishism. Transsexualism is the colloquial term for the autogynephilia paraphilia, whereby men, aroused at the fantasy of themselves as females, wear stereotypical women's clothing, specifically undergarments, to satisfy a sexual compulsion. This used to happen in private. When pharmacology and technology made it possible for the tiny number of men with this fetish to escalate their behaviors to appropriate surgically constructed facsimiles of female biology, or synthetic sex characteristics, transsexualism took root in the medical industry.

As the technology and pharmaceuticals to perform more realistic synthetic sex surgeries advance, society is forced by market growth to publicly accept this paraphilia and the ideology developed around it – which denies our biological reality, raising us above and uprooting us from the real world. A paraphilia of adult men is a difficult sell but wrapped in human rights and co-opting the natural rebelliousness of youth, it hits the marketing sweet spot.

Global Market Insights reports that "rising cases of gender dysphoria and robust advancements in sex reassignment procedures will drive the market outlook." Further, they state that "the introduction of new government policies that support sex reassignment surgery should motivate a large section of the population to opt for these procedures." Augmenting humanity in this way is on the rise because it is possible. The positive promotion of these surgeries – for which our societies are being overhauled – is driving demand. Advances in AI, genetics, data collection, biotech, reproductive technology, and neurological implants, happening in tandem with the marketing of body dissociation to youth, will see greater profits for the techno-medical complex and more intimate intrusions into our biology in the future.

When the rebranding of transsexualism marketed to children was initially launched a decade ago, it was framed as a treatment for body dysphoria, a health issue previously affecting a minuscule part of the population. The more it was promoted in the mainstream media, the more rapid the rise in children claiming an alternate sex identity. It was quickly framed as a progressive, desirable, and edgy lifestyle for youth. Young women who have undergone mastectomies of their healthy breasts are posing for corporate advertisements for underwear, shaving cream, sneakers, and feminine product lines as well as walking fashion runways and appearing on the cover of *Vogue*. An environment of threat has taken root for anyone who won't accept the narrative that this is a human right.

Why are governments rapidly overhauling societies grounded in acknowledging the reality of our species' sexual dimorphism to accommodate what was once a tiny fraction of men with a paraphilia? Autogynephilia – or more colloquially, transsexualism – reduces women's wholly sexed humanity to purchasable parts to assuage men's fixations. It has been rebranded to 'transgenderism' to groom youth into body dissociation, opening them to commercialization and experimentation for the engineering of our species' evolution.

There has never been a purported human rights movement that's gained the support of the corporate world, governments, and the financial industry like what's now framed as 'new sexes'. Over a decade, the philanthropic, political, legal, and human rights structures, the tech industry, and the largest financial houses in the world have supported special rights for people who claim a synthetic sex identity, an identity made possible by the techno-medical complex that both profits off them and uses the lesbian, gay, and bisexual human rights frame to drive a narrative of progressiveness.

The end of humanity

When sex is abolished as a meaningful category, so is humanity as we know it. This is the point of the burgeoning gender industry. Beyond profiteering, of which there is plenty, with newly constructed identities requiring a lifetime of medical attention and technologically-assisted reproduction once child patients are sterilized – it grooms the public. It assesses their acceptance of biomedical intrusions that change how we see ourselves. Will people accept the abuse of children's sex if they believe it's in good faith? How far can we go with our techno-medical intrusions into humans and the attack on women's humanity as wholly sexed beings different from men?

In a landscape where technological reproduction reigns, having sex for recreation will be the sole objective of the sex act – for as long as we are still human. This landscape is being cultivated by men with fetishes promoted by the highest levels of government and whose goal is to change laws about what constitutes manhood and womanhood. Men like Rachel Levine, Sam Brinton, Danica Roem, and Petra De Sutter are figureheads to help groom us as citizens into abolishing the sex boundary between men and women.

To believe that all our institutions and laws are being rapidly changed because powerful corporate entities care about people who have body dysmorphia is an absurdity so great that in believing it, we might as well live inside a global cult. We are so ensconced in a corporately-constructed virtual reality in which some people live outside the parameters of our sexually dimorphic species, that we can't see we have been indoctrinated.

Martine Rothblatt, the American entrepreneur and self-declared transsexual transhumanist who believes transgenderism is the on-ramp to transhumanism, is a man with a plan to deconstruct sexual dimorphism toward an end goal of lifting humans out of their biology and creating God with technology. He co-mingles with those at the highest echelons of politics, technology, biopharmaceuticals, Hollywood, and the LGBT business network.

In 2016, he lectured in Canada on the need for 'tech transhumanists' to "create a political apparatus comparable to WPATH" (World Professional Association of Transgender Health). He suggested this will establish social validity for "tech transhumanists" in the way WPATH has done for "tech transgenders." Rothblatt, also a lawyer, created the first legal framework for passing gender bills worldwide. He worked for NASA and he helped on the Human Genome Project at the UN level. He owns a biopharmaceutical corporation, a xenotransplantation farm, and a 3D organ printing corporation, and he has created a religion of disembodiment with his mentor William Sims Bainbridge. He has built a robot of his wife and lectures broadly on the melding of humanity with, and the sentience of, AI.

Rothblatt has been writing about the changes to humanity that will deconstruct sexual dimorphism since 1995. He likens sexual dimorphism to South African Apartheid. He has written about the technological future of reproduction, where humans, melded to technology, will not need to copulate.

Heather Brunskell-Evans, an academic philosopher in the UK, reported in 2021 a quote by Gendered Intelligence (GI), a global 'transgender' lobby group advocating children should be liberated to manipulate their sex characteristics. GI asserts that freedom for children and young people lies in "dismantling the culturally ascribed power of the biological." This is a fascinating statement. The message from GI seems clear: the biological reality of sex is a social construct, one now perceived to wield too much power.

A recently published UK Ministry of Defence report details advances in human augmentation, not just as they pertain to the Ministry of Defence but to our lives as human beings. It states:

> Human augmentation has the potential to impact every facet of our lives and even change the meaning of what it means to be human. It could challenge philosophical concepts, our belief systems, and ethical and legal frameworks in ways we have not anticipated.

Aren't we witnessing those changes now, in the new industry of gender, framed as a human rights movement? When discussing puberty blockers – drugs which have been shown to cause irreversible harm – Gendered Intelligence states, "It is important that children and young people … can experiment, change their mind, try out new styles, express themselves." They are advocating for children to have free rein in choosing to augment their sex characteristics and to use dangerous drugs to do so. Laws are being rapidly adjusted across many countries simultaneously, aided by LGBT NGOs, billionaires, and 'transgender' organizations, to make legal adjustments allowing for the depathologization of disembodiment.

Follow the trail

President Biden signed a bill in 2021 in which 'gender identity' will override the sex-based rights of women. Language is being manipulated to obscure the sexed reality of men and women. Is it plausible that Biden doesn't understand what he is doing? Biden was Vice President under Obama, financially assisted into office by the Pritzkers, one of the wealthiest families in the world. Jennifer Pritzker, one of the elite Pritzkers, is a man posing as a woman.

Along with his family, he has spent millions of dollars to overhaul our institutions and social structures to redefine sex as a feeling. Obama was the first president to use the word *transgender* in a State of the Union address. He also called a special meeting for 'transgender' students at the White House in 2015, earning him the title of 'Trans President'.

The corporate abolition of our sexed reality paves the way for humanity unmoored from the universe's physical laws. It projects us into a virtual reality of which we are now on the precipice, where we are not a sexually dimorphic species. Zoltan Istvan, former presidential candidate and transhumanist, stated that "A great transhumanist war will occur between those who embrace radical technology in their bodies and those who don't … Those that side with technology and AI will win." In 2015, he waxed philosophical, and falsely teamed sexual orientation with transhumanist disembodiment. He stated:

> Frankly, I could see many humans in the future stopping physical sex altogether as cranial implant technology finds precisely the right means to stimulate erogenous zones in the brain – something researchers are already working on. Real sex will probably not be able to match direct and scientifically targeted stimulation of our minds. Such actions may lead to a society where male and female traits disappear as pleasure becomes 'on-demand', and gene therapy is able to combine the most functional parts of both genders into one entity. Not surprisingly, some institutions like marriage may end up going the way of the dinosaurs.

Bainbridge, Rothblatt, De Sutter, Pritzker, and Istvan are part of a growing trend of high-profile transsexuals and technophiles grooming us for virtual reality beyond our current evolution in the biosphere. Mark Zuckerberg, Ray Kurzweil, Elon Musk, Yuval Harari, Joe Rogan, and Peter Thiel are just a handful of high-profile men who have foretold – some with alarm, others with satisfaction – that we will be pushed to evolve toward a disembodied state in fusion with AI. With societies and laws rapidly changing to obliterate sex and children used as medical fodder to obliterate the boundary of the sexes, it's time we took them seriously.

#15

Rachel Levine is a quack promoted by pharma-backed group to normalize disembodiment[15]

Secretary of Health, Dr Rachel Levine, speaking at a virtual press conference. The Pennsylvania Department of Health, 20 March 2020.

How does a dangerous man like Dr Rachel Levine wind up in the White House, spewing potentially deadly information to the public about drugs to treat children distressed about their sexed bodies? He was backed by The Victory Institute, which works to get LGBT activists into top levels of power in the US.

According to the group's website: "When LGBT presidential appointees are empowered, they can significantly influence the

---

15 First published 2 August 2022 in *Human Events*. <https://humanevents. com/2022/08/02/rachel-levine-is-a-quack-promoted-by-pharma-backed-group- to-normalize-disembodiment>

policies and direction of agencies and the executive branch to make positive change for LGBT people."

Read: In this instance, push forward gender identity industry policies and laws that harm children and profit the medical industrial complex by promoting dissociation from one's sexed body as progressive.

Levine is exactly what the Victory Institute is looking for, and during his stint as Biden's Assistant Secretary of Health and Human Services, he worked to press the administration, and the nation, into accepting the idea that children can change their sex. This despite findings that show unequivocally the dangers, both of the drugs used to halt puberty, and the life-altering, reproductive-ending effects of surgeries. Levine transitioned later in life, after fathering children, a lengthy marriage, and a long medical career.

Levine, a man with a paraphilia who compulsively objectifies womanhood, reducing their sexed humanity to parts, told the US public on July 18 2022 that kids needed to be empowered to change their sex. He touted this as 'gender affirmation' care – a euphemism for invasive medical procedures on children's sex, which are known to have harmful and long-lasting effects on their health.

The Food and Drug Administration, run by Levine's Department of Health and Human Services, had only a few weeks earlier identified that puberty blockers carry a risk of brain damage to children. It's not possible that Levine, a pediatrician, was unaware of this. These known side effects in adults were reported at least as early as 1996, when women with endometriosis and men with late-stage prostate cancer prescribed the drug were reported to present with the same side effects. Dr Laidlaw, an endocrinologist in Rocklin, California, has spoken about the dangers of these unapproved drugs for children for years.

Levine's paraphilia, colloquially known as transsexualism, has been rebranded to transgenderism for today's youth to open markets in the medical manipulations of sex. Normalizing this paraphilia, with the escalating prominence of the men who have it at all fronts of society, along with media promotion of it as progressive, edgy, cool, and part of a human rights movement, serves to drive further investments by elites in clinics to manipulate sex characteristics and assisted fertility treatments that will be needed later in life by children who are now being sterilized and otherwise harmed by these drugs. This industry is a direct outgrowth of the creation of synthetic sex characteristics that mimic women's biology for men to assuage their fetish.

Launched in 1993, the Victory Institute purportedly works to achieve and sustain global equality for people identifying as LGBT. This is done through leadership development and training to increase the number of openly LGBT elected and appointed officials at all levels of government. The Victory Institute has expanded its programming to include the Presidential Appointments Initiative, which works to place openly LGBT appointees in pro-equality presidential administrations.

Levine is a man functioning within the confines of his sexual compulsion of autogynephilia. He is a product of these efforts by the Victory Institute to put men with this paraphilia in positions of power.

According to the LGBT Victory Institute, in November 2020, they and their partners "were working with the transition team to field and identify potential candidates for appointed positions in the Biden-Harris administration." The group further explained that their goals included pressing the Biden administration to have an LGBT cabinet member, an LGBT Supreme Court justice, 'transgender ambassadors', and advocating that "openly LGBT people receive equitable representation among presidential appointees."

The 'pressing' comes from the financial clout of the medical industrial complex. The Arcus Foundation is an American LGBT non-governmental organization (NGO) whose founder is heir to Stryker Medical, a $133.55 billion (figure updated in April 2024) corporation with 54 branches in 75 countries (figures updated in April 2024). Jon Stryker funds his LGBT NGO directly from his stock in the Stryker medical corporation.

He is poised to profit from driving gender identity ideology and normalizing the myth that humans can change sex with medical technology and pharmaceuticals. The Arcus Foundation has funded Victory Institute with $10 million since 2004.

Victory Institute's sponsorship list looks like a who's who of funding to normalize synthetic sex identities, including Jon Stryker (aside from his foundation funding), Tim Gill and his LGBT NGO, Gill Foundation, Tides Foundation, Unilever, and Pfizer – one of the largest multi-national biopharma corporations worth nearly $52 billion and invested in vaccines, gene therapy and genetics – Planned Parenthood, the Human Rights Campaign, and RBC Capital Markets – a global investment bank providing services in banking, finance, and capital markets to corporations, institutional investors, asset managers and governments globally, with locations spanning 70 offices in 15 countries across North America, the UK, Europe, and the Asia-Pacific region.

Google, Gilead, Comcast, AT&T, David Geffen, Jennifer Pritzker, and David Bohnett, to name a few, are also supporting synthetic sex identities as progressive and also fund Victory Institute.

In February of 2020, during Levine's Senate confirmation hearings, he refused to answer the targeted questions of Senator Rand Paul on the issue of whether children should be allowed to make medical decisions about their sexed bodies without parental consent. Levine used an evasive statement suggesting that 'gender medicine' is too complicated a field to provide an immediate answer as to whether children should be receiving life-altering drugs and surgeries without parental consent.

Levine repeated this answer twice after being asked to clarify it the first time and completely failed to substantiate his position that children should be able to make these decisions. Now, a year and a half later, Levine is backing procedures that are known to cause permanent and long-standing harm to children and teens.

Quoted in The New Civil Rights Movement, Annise Parker, the former Houston mayor who now serves as President and CEO of the LGBT Victory Institute, in a statement said:

> Rachel Levine's nomination is groundbreaking and shows the Biden administration will choose the most qualified individuals to lead our nation regardless of sexual orientation or gender identity. Dr Levine is making history and will transform Americans' perceptions of 'trans' people when she takes office and begins to work on their behalf.

The drive to normalize synthetic sex identities under a human rights framework is a flagrant deception by the techno-medical complex to open markets in surgeries, drugs, and assisted fertility procedures for a generation of children they are sterilizing with puberty blockers.

Men like Rachel Levine, driven by this paraphilia to appropriate womanhood to assuage their compulsion, are given free rein in society to promote their paraphilia as healthy human expression. This has burgeoned into an industry where female reproductive capacity is being usurped by the techno-medical complex for profit.

The men with this compulsion are being placed by elites via organizations like the Victory Institute in positions of power and prominence to normalize this industry which creates synthetic facsimiles of human sex characteristics for marketing while transferring more and more women's reproductive labor to the tech sector.

#16

Beth Brooke-Marciniak: Promoting 'inclusivity' at the expense of women's rights[16]

The contradiction between Beth Brooke-Marciniak's advocacy for women's rights and her support for 'diversity and inclusion' policies couldn't be starker.

The political fight for male bodied people to define themselves as female, the systematic deconstruction of biological sex in language, law, on official documents, and in many of our institutions, in the name of 'inclusiveness', has been at the forefront of western cultures for nearly a decade. 'Gender Identity' and 'Transgenderism', for which 'inclusiveness' has become corporate and institutional shorthand, have become common expressions, even if most people are still not sure exactly what they mean. The financial force being used by corporations, billionaire philanthropists and governments to dictate this deconstruction of sexual dimorphism in society cannot co-exist with women's sex-based rights. They are mutually exclusive.

The world's most powerful woman in a world without females

No one exemplifies the contradiction of the current political fight for the institutionalization of 'transgender' mythology and women's sex-based rights quite like Beth Brooke-Marciniak, named one of Forbes "World's 100 Most Powerful Women" ten times.

---

16   First published 17 April 2020, *Uncommon Ground Media*. <https://uncommon groundmedia.com/beth-brooke-marciniak-promoting-inclusivity-at-the-expense-of-womens-rights/>

As former head of public policy at the professional services firm Ernst & Young (EY), Brooke-Marciniak was responsible for helping to influence policies related to global capital markets. Formerly with the US Department of the Treasury, responsible for all tax policy matters related to insurance and managed care, playing roles in the healthcare reform and Superfund reform efforts, we can see how she earned such accolades.

Brooke-Marciniak serves on the board of Vital Voices Global Partnership, an American international non-profit, that works with women leaders in the areas of economic empowerment, women's political participation, and human rights. The organization is headquartered in Washington, D.C. She co-chairs the International Council on Women's Business Leadership. She also sits on the boards of the Aspen Institute and the Women's Advisory Board of the World Economic Forum. Her accomplishments for women's promotion in society are vast and admirable.

Beth A. Brooke-Marciniak, Global Vice-Chair, Public Policy, Ernst & Young, USA and Shamina Singh, Executive Director, MasterCard Center for Inclusive Growth, MasterCard, USA. Moderated by Oliver Cann, Head of Media Content, World Economic Forum, 20–23 January 2016.

As an out and married lesbian, Brooke-Marciniak has simultaneously used her power and influence to move forward the corporate agenda for LGBT diversity and inclusion. 'Diversity and Inclusion' is a political agenda that has moved beyond the rights of lesbians, gays, and bisexuals to have same-sex relationships while having their civil liberties protected within employment and social structures, to driving a biology-denying ideology using a civil-rights framework through the culture. Under the banner of 'gender identity' or LGBTQI+, a panoply of sexual disorders, fetishes, post-modern deconstructionism and gender bending have been situated and conflated with LGB civil rights, in an effort to deconstruct sexual dimorphism. This conflation is creating a vast array of identities divorced from sexual dimorphism, purportedly needing protection under the law, and more importantly, creating marketing opportunities for corporations and the medical industrial complex at the expense of women's reality as one half of a sexually dimorphic species. If men can legally be women, then women cease to exist as a category. If females cease to exist as one half of a sexually dimorphic species, then their ability to fight for their sex-based rights becomes null and void.

The promotion of female athletes in a world without women

From such an accomplished background, one can see the fervor Brooke-Marciniak has for women's sex-based social equality. Being a skilled sportswoman during her years at Purdue University, her interest in empowering other female athletes stands at the fore of her accomplishments and her writing. She has been inducted into the Indiana Basketball Hall of Fame and received the Theodore Roosevelt Award, the top individual honor bestowed by the US National Collegiate Athletic Association (NCAA). In January 2019, Brooke-Marciniak was appointed to the United States Olympic and Paralympic Committee board of directors and began serving as an independent director.

In 2013, while at EY, Brooke-Marciniak founded Women Athletes Business Network (WABN), a unique program designed to assist elite female athletes seeking to make the transition from sport to successful careers in business and leadership. Simultaneously, she was also head of inclusiveness and diversity at the global firm, where she spearheaded the creation of their Corporate Responsibility group and promoted 'gender identity mythology'. Six years later, Olympians Martina Navratilova and Sharron Davies had to make a concerted appeal to the Olympics, other sports organizations and the media, to get men out of women's sports when stories were being printed and policies were being adopted that validated men as women.

In 2018, Brooke-Marciniak was named Global Advocate of the Year by the National LGBT Chamber of Commerce for her work to champion LGBTI issues on a global scale. She was also Co-Chair for Partnership for Global LGBTI Equality, and she sits on the board of OUTLeadership, an organization driving 'gender identity' mythology globally.

Brooke-Marciniak's efforts for women's empowerment within society and sports, alongside her work for acceptance of the biology-denying mythology of 'gender identity', expose the schism at the heart of 'diversity and inclusion' policies. Brooke-Marciniak, and many like her, are caught in the conundrum that the current LGBTQI+ represents, especially how they cancel out the sex-based rights of females. You cannot protect sex-based rights, or rights based in same-sex attraction, while simultaneously deconstructing sex within the law.

The inclusivity schism of LGBTQI+

All Brooke-Marciniak's efforts to empower women disappear when women have to fight for their privacy, corporate, institutional, political and athletic positions anew, while men who claim to be women insert themselves into those positions in the name of 'gender identity'.

Women's organizations and corporate products that serve women's specific biological needs, such as midwives associations and family planning organizations, under financial coercion by the gender lobby, have erased the use of female to denote biologically female processes, such as breast-feeding, pregnancy, birth, abortion, menstruation, etc. Birth certificates can now be changed in many US states to adhere to a person's feeling about themselves, overriding their actual biology. The same can be said for drivers' licenses. What is being erased by the 'gender identity' movement is sexual dimorphism, to be replaced by an individual's relationships to sex stereotypes and how they want to be perceived by others.

Brooke-Marciniak and those she exemplifies, fighting simultaneously for women's rights and 'gender identity', cannot have it both ways. Either women exist as one-half of a sexually dimorphic species that are naturally and culturally vulnerable to the other half of this sexually dimorphic species because of their biology and their social standing, or sex and women do not exist and thereby need no protections, which would amount to a large-scale waste of time for Brooke-Marciniak and the pursuits she has mastered over the course of her life to assure women social and professional parity with men.

#17

The rich Canadian philanthropist driving body dissociation[17]

In America, there are rich transsexual and gay men at the helm of the gender industry, many of whom I have written about in these posts. These (mostly) men, and their collective wealth, are driving a narrative through the USA and other western societies that sexual dimorphism is not real. They have captured human rights organizations, academia, sports associations, the media, and medical institutions, and are forcing their biology-denying, fetishizing ideology into children's school curriculums and libraries and corporate culture.

Like Jon Stryker, founder of the Arcus Foundation in the USA, the largest LGBT NGO in the world, Canada has its own rich, gay, male philanthropist, who emerged out of the financial industry and is driving gender ideology in his own country and beyond. Mark S. Bonham was included in the 2017 OUTstanding LGBT Business Leaders' list, sharing accolades from the organization, with Martine Rothblatt, the transsexual transhumanist at the heart of the gender industry, and Mark Zuckerberg, the transhumanist and CEO of Facebook. Bonham was awarded OUTstanding Philanthropist of the Year in 2018 by the Association of Fundraising Professionals. He has had an elaborate career in the Canadian financial industry and received his Master of Science in Economics, with a focus on Capital Market Theory, from the London School of Economics.

Bonham has provided millions of dollars in funding to LGBT issues in Canada, including but not limited to Egale Centre, the city of Toronto's first LGBT homeless youth shelter and The Casey House Hospital (an AIDS-specialty hospital) in Toronto. He is the

---

17   First published 6 November 2021. <https://www.the11thhourblog.com/post/the-rich-canadian-philanthropist-driving-body-dissociation>

author of three LGBT books to date: *A Path to Diversity: LGBTQ Participation in the Working World* (2017); *Notables: 101 Global LGBTQ People who Changed the World* (2015) and *Champions: Biographies of Global LGBTQ Pioneers* (2014).

Bonham also funded and is a co-founder and Managing Editor of the online biographical encyclopedia QueerBio.com, a source of biographical information on over 15,000 historical and contemporary LGBTQ individuals from around the world in the categories of sports, business, the arts and entertainment, literature and poetry, activists, politicians, and much more. In 2018, QueerBio.com had over six million page views. In 2016, he became manager of the Veritas Foundation, a non-profit charitable public foundation, with a mission to be Canada's authoritative source for individuals, groups and companies to participate in the country's charitable sector. Like Jon Stryker in America, he helps to guide the corporate and philanthropic donations of Canadian elites.

Bonham also created the Mark S. Bonham Centre for Sexual Diversity Studies, which has been funded by American transsexual and billionaire philanthropist, Jennifer Pritzker, who received an award for his contributions in 2016. Pritzker funded a similar program at the University of Minnesota in 2017. The Bonham Centre is the world's largest degree-granting research center on LGBT+ issues. The Pritzker family and their billions of dollars are prominent drivers of the institutionalization of gender ideology in America and the development of the body-dissociating ideology into an industry.

The Bonham Centre offers an undergraduate program, a collaborative graduate specialization (MA and PhD), hosts academic and community events, and supports research in queer, 'trans', and sexuality studies. It also sports a newly minted Queer, Trans Research Lab (QTRL).

Part of the Bonham Centre's curriculum is the Committee on Schools and Education (CSE), a school and community outreach program, which functions similarly to the GLSEN Foundation in the USA, funded by the Arcus Foundation. The founder of GLSEN,

Kevin Jennings, moved to become Executive Director at the Arcus Foundation in 2012. The CSE is composed of university scholars from diverse institutions as well as independent scholars, K-12 educators, and professionals who work in schools and community-based organizations serving children, youth and their families. A primary goal is

> to move sex education from its current focus on risk, protection, and control to a focus on the body, desire, and agency. It promotes further research into how sexuality education is currently proceeding within the confines of existing institutional and social constraints and alternative ways in which it might be re-imagined.

Nicholas Matte, a woman who thinks she's a man, is a teacher in the Sexual Diversities Studies Program at the Bonham Centre and curates the Sexual Representation Collection. Through her extensive involvement with 'trans' archiving, she also facilitates student engagement with a wide range of significant primary resources, such as the University of Victoria's 'Transgender Archives' and the Digital 'Transgender' Archives. The University of Victoria 'Trans' department is also funded by Jennifer Pritzker. Martine Rothblatt has received an honorary doctorate of law from the university, and has been a guest speaker in the 'Trans' department.

In 2016, Matte was part of a panel discussion on 'Genders, Rights and Freedom of Speech', hosted by The Agenda with Steve Paikin. Steven Paikin is a Canadian journalist, author, and documentary producer. Popular Canadian author and speaker Jordan Peterson also sat on the panel, where Matte explained to the other panelists and the host that "it is not correct that there is such a thing as biological sex; this is a misconception of 'cis' culture and institutions." She added that "there is no such a thing as male and female."

Mark Bonham, like his American counterparts driving the dismantling of sexual dimorphism through American and European institutions, is a businessman and a corporatist, not a grass roots activist. He is President of Bonham & Co. Inc. in Toronto, Ontario, a private holding company, offering investment portfolio advice to select, elite clients. His investment portfolio includes diverse industries such as FinTech, health sciences, consumer products and services, and technology.

The Bonham Centre funded the development of the Advancing Dignity Initiative (ADI) in Canada, presented in 2015, which works much like the MAP Project, founded and funded by the Arcus Foundation in the USA in 2008. The purpose of the ADI report is to

> highlight how a number of countries, including Canada, can and do use foreign policy and refugee policy to promote equality on the basis of sexual orientation, gender identity, gender expression, and intersex status.

The stated mission of MAP is

> to speed achievement of full social and political equality for LGBT people by providing donors and organizations with strategic information, insights, and analyses that help them increase and align resources for highest impact.

The ADI report funded by Bonham concludes with this commentary:

> We also note that most programming and policy work in support of the human rights of LGBTI people have focused predominantly on the rights of LGB individuals. Far more research, programming, and policy are required in order to ensure that human rights violations faced by trans individuals and intersex individuals, in particular, are afforded the attention and concern that they deserve.

The incredible danger these documents reveal are both the breadth of organizations involved in steering human sexuality and the dismantling of human sexual dimorphism, and how LGB and intersex conditions are being used as a Trojan Horse to drive an ideology of disembodiment through global institutions and governments. Most people in western societies want equal and fair treatment for same-sex attracted people. Educational efforts toward the extension of that equality are welcomed by many institutions, without consideration of what the 'T', the 'Q' and the 'I' are doing in the midst of a movement for same-sex attracted individuals.

The agenda of 'T+' is not hidden, by any means, though it may seem incredulous to the untrained eye, or for those assuming that 'T+' is an organic extension of LGB human rights. Martin/Martine Rothblatt, who created the draft for the first 'gender bill', has written and lectured extensively about the project to deconstruct human sexual dimorphism in his books, *From Transgender to Transhuman: A Manifesto on the Freedom of Form* (2011) and *Unzipped Genes: Taking Charge of Baby Making in the New Millennium* (1997). Everywhere we look in western cultures, what is being promoted as 'gender identity' is the dissolution of sexual dimorphism toward a tech-takeover of reproduction and the opening of the human body for commodification. This anti-reality ideology – now in medical schools and children's grade schools – is moving rapidly through law in western cultures. The ability to speak about these transgressions against reality are censored and framed as hate speech. We are in a fight for our lives and must accept that what we are looking at here has no relation to a human rights movement. Accepting the concept of 'transgenderism' is a death knell for humanity.

#18

The billionaire family pushing Synthetic Sex Identities (SSI)

The wealthy, powerful, and sometimes very weird
Pritzker cousins have set their sights on a new God-like goal:
Using gender ideology to remake human biology[18]

One of the most powerful yet unremarked-upon drivers of our
current wars over definitions of gender is a concerted push by
members of one of the richest families in the United States to
transition Americans from a dimorphic definition of sex to the
broad acceptance and propagation of synthetic sex identities
(SSI). Over the past decade, the Pritzkers of Illinois, who helped
put Barack Obama in the White House and include among their
number former US Secretary of Commerce, Penny Pritzker, current
Illinois Governor J. B. Pritzker, and philanthropist Jennifer Pritzker,
appear to have used a family philanthropic apparatus to drive an
ideology and practice of disembodiment into our medical, legal,
cultural, and educational institutions.

I first wrote about the Pritzkers, whose fortune originated in
the Hyatt hotel chain, and their philanthropy directed toward
normalizing what people call 'transgenderism' in 2018. I have
since stopped using the word 'transgenderism' as it has no clear
boundaries, which makes it useless for communication, and have
instead opted for the term SSI (synthetic sex identities), which
more clearly defines what some of the Pritzkers and their allies
are funding – even as it ignores the biological reality of 'male' and
'female' and 'gay' and 'straight'.

The creation and normalization of SSI speaks much more
directly to what is happening in US culture and elsewhere, under

18   First published 15 June 2022, *Tablet Magazine*. <https://www.tabletmag.com/
    sections/news/articles/billionaire-family-pushing-synthetic-sex-identities-ssi-
    pritzkers>

an umbrella of human rights. With the introduction of SSI, the current incarnation of the LGBTQ+ network – as distinct from the prior movement that fought for equal rights for gay and lesbian Americans but ended in 2020 with the finding in Bostock v. Clayton County that LGBTQ+ is a protected class for discrimination purposes – is working closely with the techno-medical complex, big banks, international law firms, pharma giants, and corporate power to solidify the idea that humans are not a sexually dimorphic species – which contradicts reality and the fundamental premises not only of 'traditional' religions but of the gay and lesbian civil rights movements and much of the feminist movement, for which sexual dimorphism and resulting gender differences are foundational premises.

Through investments in the techno-medical complex, where new highly medicalized sex identities are being conjured, the Pritzkers and other elite donors are attempting to normalize the idea that human reproductive sex exists on a spectrum. These investments go toward creating new SSI using surgeries and drugs, and by instituting rapid language reforms to prop up these new identities and induce institutions and individuals to normalize them. In 2018, for example, at the Ronald Reagan Medical Center at the University of California Los Angeles (where the Pritzkers are major donors and hold various titles), the Department of Obstetrics and Gynecology advertised several options for young females who think they can be men to have their reproductive organs removed, a procedure termed 'gender affirming care'.

The Pritzkers became the first American family to have a medical school bear its name in recognition of a private donation when it gave $12 million to the University of Chicago School of Medicine in 1968. In June 2002, the family announced an additional gift of $30 million to be invested in the University of Chicago's Biological Sciences Division and School of Medicine. These investments provided the family with a bridgehead into the world of academic medicine, which it has since expanded in pursuit of a well-defined agenda centered around SSI. Also in 2002,

Jennifer Pritzker founded the Tawani Foundation, which has since provided funding to Howard Brown Health and Rush Memorial Medical Center in Chicago, the University of Arkansas for Medical Sciences Foundation Fund, and the University of Minnesota's Institute for Sexual and Gender Health, all of which provide some version of 'gender care'. In the case of the latter, 'clients' include "gender creative children as well as transgender and gender non-conforming adolescents ..."

In 2012, J. B. Pritzker and his wife, M. K. Pritzker, worked with The Bridgespan Group – a management consultancy to nonprofits and philanthropists – to develop a long-term strategy for the J. B and M. K. Pritzker Family Foundation. Their work together included conducting research on developments in the field of early childhood education, to which the foundation committed $25 million.

Ever since, a motivating and driving force behind the Pritzkers' family-wide commitment to SSI has been J. B.'s cousin Jennifer (born James) Pritzker – a retired lieutenant colonel in the Illinois Army National Guard and the father of three children. In 2013, around the time gender ideology reached the level of mainstream US culture, Jennifer Pritzker announced a transition to womanhood. Since then, Pritzker has used the Tawani Foundation to help fund various institutions that support the concept of a spectrum of human sexes, including the Human Rights Campaign Foundation, the Williams Institute UCLA School of Law, the National Center for Transgender Equality, the Transgender Legal Defense and Education Fund, the American Civil Liberties Union, the Palm Military Center, the World Professional Association of Transgender Health (WPATH), and many others. Tawani Enterprises, the private investment counterpart to the philanthropic foundation, invests in and partners with Squadron Capital LLC, a Chicago-based private investment vehicle that has acquired a number of medical device companies that manufacture instruments, implants, cutting tools, and injection molded plastic products for use in surgeries. As in the case of Jon Stryker, founder of the LGBT mega-NGO, the Arcus

Foundation, it is hard to avoid the impression of complementarity between Jennifer Pritzker's for-profit medical investments and philanthropic support for SSI.

Pritzker also helps fund the University of Minnesota National Center for Gender Spectrum Health, which claims that

> the gender spectrum is inclusive of the wide array of gender identities beyond binary definitions of gender – inclusive of cisgender and transgender identities, gender queer, and nonbinary identities as a normal part of the natural expression of gender. Gender spectrum health is the healthy, affirmed, positive development of a gender identity and expression that is congruent with the individual's sense of self.

The university, where Pritzker has served on the Leadership Council for the Program in Human Sexuality, provides 'young adult gender services' in the medical school's Institute for Sexual and Gender Health.

Pritzker's philanthropy is also active in Canada, where Jennifer has helped fund the University of Toronto's Bonham Centre for Sexual Diversity Studies, a teaching institution invested in the deconstruction of human sex. An instructor in the Bonham Centre and the curator of its Sexual Representation Collection – "Canada's largest archival collection of pornography" – is transgender studies professor Nicholas Matte who denies categorically that sexual dimorphism exists. Pritzker also created the first chair in transgender studies at the University of Victoria in British Columbia. The current chair, Aaron Devor, founded an annual conference called Moving Trans History Forward, whose keynote speaker in 2016 was the renowned transhumanist, Martine Rothblatt, who was mentored by the transhumanist Ray Kurzweil of Google. Rothblatt lectured there on the value of creating an organization such as WPATH to serve 'tech transgenders' in the cultivation of 'tech transhumanists'. (Rothblatt's ideology of disembodiment and technological religion seems to be having nearly as much influence on American culture as Sirius satellite radio, which Rothblatt co-founded.) Rothblatt is an integral presence at OUTLeadership, a business networking arm of the LGBTQ+ movement, and appears to believe that "we are making God as we are implementing technology that is ever more all-knowing, ever-present, all-powerful, and beneficent."

For-profit medical corporations and nonprofit institutions that intersect with the goliath LGBT NGO infrastructure, many of which receive Pritzker funding, have created a political scaffolding to engineer the institutionalization of SSI ideology and medical practice in the United States – solidifying the concept of people being born in wrongly sexed bodies or wrongly being born in sexed bodies at all. At least two clinics in California are now providing non-binary surgeries and nullification surgeries for individuals who feel both male and female, or like neither.

The Gender Multispeciality Service (GeMS) at Boston Children's Hospital, "the first major program in the US to focus on gender-diverse and transgender adolescents," was founded in 2007. "Since that time," says the GeMS website, "we have expanded our program to welcome patients from ages 3 to 25." The first such clinic for children in the Midwest, the Gender and Sex Development Program at Lurie Children's Hospital, opened in Chicago in 2013 with a $500,000 initial donation from Jennifer Pritzker; in 2016, Pritzker donated another $500,000. (The husband of Jean 'Gigi' Pritzker, another cousin, sits on Lurie's board of directors.) The Gender Mapping Project estimates that there are now thousands of similar 'gender clinics' around the world, and over 400 that offer to medically manipulate the sex of children.

Like Stryker's Arcus Foundation, the Pritzkers have forged a close relationship with the psychiatric establishment. The Pritzker Department of Psychiatry and Behavioral Health at Lurie was launched with a $15 million gift from the Pritzker Foundation in 2019, and received another $6.45 million in 2022 to address "concerns about mental health consequences for children and adolescents arising from the COVID pandemic." Illinois Gov. J. B. Pritzker, Jennifer's cousin, signed into law SB 2085, Coverage of the Psychiatric Collaborative Care Model (CoCM) – the American Psychiatric Association's model legislation requiring private insurers and Medicaid in Illinois to cover CPT codes for CoCM, which

> requires a primary care (or other) physician or clinician to lead a team that includes a behavioral health care manager who checks in with patients at least once a month and an off-site psychiatric consultant who regularly reviews patients' progress and offers advice.

Jeanne Pritzker, married to J. B.'s brother Anthony, who is Jennifer's cousin, is a training psychologist at UCLA where she and her husband established the Anthony and Jeanne Pritzker Family Scholarship to support medical students at UCLA's David Geffen School of Medicine. Mrs Pritzker is a member of the Board of Visitors at the Geffen School, which is affiliated with a children's hospital named after Mattel – the multinational toy company that debuted a 'transgender Barbie' recently made in the likeness of the actor Laverne Cox.

On June 30, 2019, Gov. Pritzker issued Executive Order 19–11, titled 'Strengthening Our Commitment to Affirming and Inclusive Schools', to welcome and support children with manufactured sex identities. A task force was established to outline statewide criteria for schools and teachers that recommended districts amend their school board policies "to strengthen protections for transgender, nonbinary, and gender nonconforming students."

In August 2021, Gov. Pritzker signed into law a new sex education bill for all public schools in Illinois, the first of its kind designed in accordance with the second edition of the National Sex Education Standards (NSES) to update sex ed. curricula in K-12 schools. Bill SB0 818 will be implemented on or before 1 August 2022. Though the bill includes a written opt-out for parents (but not an alternative if they do opt-out), many are concerned with the material being brought into children's schools under the auspices of teaching them sexual health – namely gender identity ideology and other related material.

The NSES manual was crafted by The Future of Sex Education Initiative (FoSE) and funded by the Grove Foundation which in turn has also worked with the David and Lucile Packard Foundation (of Hewlett-Packard fortune) and Ford Foundation to institute Working to Institutionalize Sex Education (WISE) – "A national initiative that supports school districts in implementing sex education" –throughout the country. The Bridgespan Group, which assisted the Pritzkers with their philanthropic trajectory in 2012, was retained by the Packard Foundation to review its collaborative efforts across its investment portfolio and to report on a series of case studies, including the WISE initiative.

FoSE is a collaboration between three other organizations: The Sexuality Information and Education Council of the United States (SIECUS), "a national, nonprofit organization dedicated to affirming that sexuality is a natural and healthy part of life"; Advocates for Youth, "partnering with youth leaders, adult allies, and youth-serving organizations to advocate for policies and champion programs that recognize young people's rights to honest sexual health information"; and Answer, "which provides and promotes unfettered access to comprehensive sexuality education for young people." Each of these is also funded by the Grove Foundation, whose fortune comes from the now-deceased Andrew Grove, former CEO of Intel Corporation.

FoSE has created a 'scaffolding approach' to teaching kids about sex in public schools and teaching them very young. Its credo is that not only are younger children able to discuss sexuality-related issues, but that the early grades may, in fact, be the best time to introduce topics related to sexual orientation, gender identity, and expression, gender equality, and social justice related to the LGBTQ community before hetero- and cisnormative values and assumptions become more deeply ingrained and less mutable.

Critics of the NSES standards created by the FoSE collaborative and now being implemented in Illinois under Gov. Pritzker may have concerns about a 72-page manual in which the term 'anal sex' comes up ten times and the word 'intimacy' only half as often. The word 'gender', for what it's worth, is used 270 times. While many Americans are still trying to understand why women are being erased in language and law, and why children are being taught they can choose their sex, the Pritzker cousins and others may be well on their way to engineering a new way to be human. But what could possibly explain the abrupt drive of wealthy elites to deconstruct who and what we are and to manipulate children's sex characteristics in clinics now spanning the globe while claiming new rights for those being deconstructed? Perhaps it is profit. Perhaps it is the pleasure of seeing one's own personal obsessions writ large. Perhaps it is the human temptation to play God. No matter what the answer is, it seems clear that SSI will be an enduring part of America's future.

#19

'Gender identity': A corporate fiction[19]

There is zero difference between people being called 'transgender' and the rest of us, in the sense that we're all biological and exist as part of a sexually dimorphic species. We're all tethered to reality by our sex. The mysterious otherworldliness created around people who attempt to medically disown their sex is a corporate construction, a fiction. It is purposeful, powerful, and dangerous.

The creation of this corporate fiction is one step toward attempting to overlay a virtual reality onto the natural world and to construct a religion out of technology. Elites at the highest levels of our technocracy have been speaking about technologies so advanced that they provide us with god-like qualities for at least fifty years, probably longer.

---

19 First published 10 December 2022. <https://jbilek.substack.com/p/gender-identity-a-corporate-fiction>

The current iteration of this ideology, established by the technocracy we live in, is meant to ensconce us in a virtual or cyber world to which the natural world is subjugated. With its massive propaganda apparatus, it has only taken a decade to convince the populace that there is a unique type of human, untethered to the biosphere like the rest of us mere 'biological people'.

The political left (media and politicians) is helping to manifest this virtual reality driving a narrative of unique, ethereal humans, unattached to the ecosystem and needing special rights within law and society.

The political right (media and politicians) is linguistically supporting this edifice whenever they argue that 'transgender women' don't belong in 'biological women's' sports, prisons, colleges, etc. They solidify the illusion of another type of human that is not biological at every turn. Until the media focuses on tearing down the faulty premise of people outside of the parameters of our sexed reality, this exercise of building a virtual reality for us to live in will only continue to be solidified. The premise of alternate humans must be attacked along with the political lobby fostering the illusion.

Corporations, banks, international investment houses, governments, legal institutions, and influential non-governmental organizations (NGOs) market the idea that we are not a sexually dimorphic species. They don't care about the identity issues of a minuscule part of the population. It is patently ridiculous to think so. They are marketing disembodiment. 'Gender', currently being promoted as a revolutionary human rights movement to set us free, is an industry posing as social progress for the people. It seeks to deconstruct human reproductive sex for profit and human engineering. It is posited that our freedom will emerge when technology takes over where human reproduction ends. When this purported dead weight of human reproduction ends, male and female will be obsolete. We can then live as our 'authentic selves' beyond male and female, youth and adult, beyond material existence and its limitations.

Our sex is being commodified, reduced to parts, toward this end. This occurs via the normalization of the male sexual fetish of transsexualism being promoted corporately and the appropriation of medical, synthetic simulacrums of women's wholly sexed humanity. The term 'transgender' is a rebranding of this fetish and works as an ad campaign for this burgeoning industry. The 'trans' flag is its logo – which is why it replaced the POW flag at the White House during 'trans' awareness week in 2019. It's why we see it everywhere. The wares this industry traffics in are uteruses, sperm, ovaries, eggs, and synthetic facsimiles of penises, breasts, and vaginas. There are now international forums promoting these wares, AI facial mapping, genetic screening, remaking of the human body, and lawyering to make all the transactions tidy. Investors are lining up. Women are being systematically reduced, in language and law, to 'cervix havers', 'menstruators', 'gestators', and 'bleeders' because they have the lion's share of responsibility for the reproduction of our species which technocratic elites are attempting to colonize.

The male sexual fetish of transsexualism, a compulsion to own female biology for oneself, has been rebranded as 'transgenderism' because a male fetish would be a tough sell to any population. 'Transgender' sounds cool and edgy and feels mutinous for teens filled with the rebellious spirit of youth who are clueless about the repercussions of being sterilized by the drugs and surgeries being marketed to them. Claiming synthetic sex, a corporately manufactured illusion has become the medical-tech generation's counterpart to getting a secret tattoo. These kids adopting synthetic sex identities have grown up online with cyber identities and have had their personalities medicalized since they were old enough to talk, while previous generations were out exploring the real world. They and their parents have been fed an array of disorders and cures, from attention deficit/hyperactivity disorder (ADHD), borderline personality disorder, autism, anxiety, oppositional defiance disorder, depression, and everything in between. Medical intervention in their lives and personalities is not strange to them. It has been normalized. Many of these disorders have real and painful consequences, but they are also manifesting in societies that are broken, dissociated, and in a world that has been poisoned.

The communication now brought to the medical industry's generation of children is that some humans are untethered to the biosphere (they are otherworldly people). This message is being propagated over all mainstream media by both the political left and the political right. It is being driven into children's schools by rich, influential people and organizations with deep connections to the techno-medical complex. These messages were not here ten years ago. In the past decade, there has been a deluge of media propaganda selling us all on the idea that there are biological men and women and then another type of human – trans-humans if you will.

International legal firms, financial investment houses, and Goliath NGOs have convinced us – or at the very least have us cowing to the concept – that people's 'authentic selves' can be born in the wrong body.

'Gender identity' ideology is not politically separate from business. Business is no longer separated from politics. We are governed by billionaires in finance who drive policy through our political and social institutions. A façade of democracy shrouds the oligarchic technocracy we live in, controlling this idea of alternate humans, just like the gender performances in gender ideology shroud the corporate profiteering from the colonization of human reproductive sex for profit and human engineering.

As reported recently by Gender Dissent (GD), an organization exposing the money and influence behind the gender industry in Canada, this process has been helped by cloaking corporatism in a human rights frame.

In their report, GD elucidated a human rights document called the Yogyakarta Principles (YP), devised in 2006 and updated in 2017, to drive the concept of gender identity into law, reducing humans' wholly sexed humanity to interchangeable commodities.

Principle 31 promotes that governments "end the registration of the sex and gender of persons in their identity documents."

The original 29 signatories of the Yogyakarta Principles were brought together in 2006 by the Canadian company Allied Rainbow Communities International (ARC International), also reported on by GD, which sent them to Yogyakarta, Indonesia, to craft the principles.

GD clarifies, "the principles are not a UN document and have never been discussed or ratified by any UN body." Their report includes a document detailing how they came to be created.

ARC is funded by the Arcus Foundation, the most significant LGBT NGO in America with global reach. Its funding mechanism is contingent on grantees adopting the concept of 'gender ideology', a complete myth dropped into western cultures a decade ago and driven by money and propaganda. In a 2008 meeting in Bellagio, Italy, the Arcus Foundation hosted 29 leaders in global philanthropy that helped steer the YP and 'gender identity' into the UN and western governments. Millions of dollars of medical corporation money fuel the Arcus Foundation. Jon Stryker is the foundation's founder and is heir to a multi-billion-dollar ($133.55 billion, updated April 2024) medical supply corporation, Stryker Medical. Stryker Corporation spans 75 countries. The money funneled to the Arcus Foundation and, by extension, many other foundations and organizations, give the profiteering and human engineering of the techno-medical industry in the name of 'gender identity' its veneer of human rights.

Technocratic elites have spent years discussing the virtual reality they seek to create. We will be enclosed and connected to everything and everyone else via bodiless minds without any roots in the biosphere. Elon Musk promotes his *Neuralink*, Ray Kurzweil, a *Singularity*, Martine Rothblatt's *Terasem* movement, and *Lifenaut* organizations tout immortality in cyberspace. Mark Zuckerberg promises a utopia in his Metaverse, and Yuval Harari's technological god will rid us of the cumbersome world of nature for something much more significant. Elites and corporations are investing in humans framed as otherworldly and not like the rest of us, rooted in biology, because they see profits and believe this is our future. The fascination of elites with 'gender ideology' takes on a new light when seen in context. These 'other' humans, as they are remade, each in their own image, will feed an already bloated techno-medical complex.

The changes to our biology, the way we think, and what we believe are being made manifest inside the techno-medical gulag we are ensnared in and given religious overtones by men who think they're God. Until we can unwind from the tale, we will be unable to help children who, like fish in water, simply flow with the current.

Too many of us are caught in the riptide-like tenets of this techno-religious cult already. It would be wise not to dismiss its draw. It has taken hold of many intelligent people. Inside the cult is a virtual reality with ethereal beings, and outside is real life, with real humans. We can still pull out of this cult, but each minute not spent resisting this dystopia is a moment we can't get back.

#20

Amazon, censorship and the gender industry[20]

Jeff Bezos' Amazon platform is toying with our First Amendment right to free speech.

Following on the heels of Amazon shadow banning Abigail Shrier's book, *Irreversible Damage: The Transgender Craze Seducing Our Daughters* about the transgender social contagion affecting young women, Ryan Anderson's book, *When Harry Became Sally* was banned outright by the tech giant. The book, which had previously been on Amazon's bestseller list, aimed to provide "thoughtful answers to questions arising from our transgender moment" and offered "a balanced approach to public policy on gender identity."

---

20   First published 15 April 2021, updated 15 October 2022. <https://www.the11th hourblog.com/post/amazon-censorship-and-the-gender-industry>

The Transgender Industrial Complex, reporting on the industry of gender by Scott Howard, was banned by Amazon nearly as fast as it hit the platform in 2020, though it has since reappeared. In April 2021, Amazon temporarily took down the book *Desist, Detrans, & Detox: Getting Your Child Out of the Gender Cult*, by Maria Keffler. No warning, no email, just an initial de-platforming, followed by a cryptic apology and reinstatement.

In February 2021, Amazon reported that the company's policies changed between 2018 and 2021, attempting to frame Anderson's book as offensive for referring to LGBTQ+ identities as mental illness. Anderson refuted those charges. The banning itself is a blatant attack on free speech, speech that Amazon has described as hateful, though curiously, Hitler's tome, *Mein Kampf,* didn't make the banned-for-hate cut list. Amazon holds 80% of the book market, so a ban, a shadow ban, and a de-platforming with a re-platforming can cause damage to any profits a writer may secure through book sales, not to mention their reputations. The forced loss of income and damage to writers' reputations by de-platforming their books is egregious. But banning books goes far beyond egregious into territory we should be responding to.

Beyond this tyranny and overt assault on our First Amendment rights in America, lies a darker reality yet.

Gender Identity has opened new markets for the medical industrial complex.

What happened between Ryan's publication of *When Harry Became Sally*, its best-seller status, and the subsequent removal of the book, while other books on the topic of the gender industry were also being removed and shadow banned? Let's examine.

As the gender industry is part of the medical industrial complex, we need to follow the money trail behind Amazon's decisions to censor books that might interfere with their profits.

Here are some highlights of Amazon's push into healthcare during 2019 and where they're headed:

- Teaming up with JP Morgan Chase, and Warren Buffett's Berkshire Hathaway, Amazon has set its sights on hospitals and outpatient clinics in the USA, aiming to become the leading provider of medical supplies to them.
- Amazon is among the tech giants making the biggest impact on healthcare. Coupled with its vast number of users and sellers, it can be a fertile testing ground for future healthcare applications.
- In March 2021, Amazon made a $2 million investment in Boston-based Beth Israel Deaconess Medical Center to test artificial intelligence tools.
- Amazon Web Services deepened its Next Gen Stats partnership with the NFL in December 2022 to advance player health. The partnership plans to use AWS artificial intelligence and machine learning to provide insights into player injuries and how equipment, game rules, and rehabilitation strategies can affect player health.

Since 2018, Amazon has made several significant partnerships and investments in the healthcare industry, which will likely continue into the new decade. In 2018, Amazon purchased PillPack for $753 million to enter the online pharmacy market. Amazon formed Amazon Care, an online virtual medical clinic for employees in 2019, but subsequently closed it in 2022. Later, Amazon made a second acquisition and snapped up a start-up called Health Navigator, which provides technology and services to digital health companies.

With the acquisition of PillPack and the recent release of HIPAA (The Health Insurance Portability and Accountability Act) compliant Alexa skills, analysts speculate that Amazon is preparing to disrupt the $934.8 billion global pharmaceutical industry, already allowing consumers to order and refill their prescriptions as quickly as they would buy clothing or toys off Amazon Prime and creating a full-scale pharmacy business within the Amazon infrastructure.

Unsurprisingly, as the new gender industry is poised for growth, Amazon is going all-in for employees who attempt to disown their sexed reality (as well as their new pharmaceutical consumer base), creating a guidebook of benefits for the Aetna health plans of their 'transgender employees'.

Amazon 'transgender employee' Aetna health plans cover non-surgical medical treatment such as hormone 'therapy' and mental health for minors with 'gender dysphoria' (surgical interventions are considered when individuals reach age 18).

Hormones and specialized surgical procedures for adults, such as double mastectomies, rib excision, nipple reconstruction, scrotoplasty, penectomy, vulvectomy, orchiectomy, vaginectomy, etc., are all covered. Amazon-Aetna also offers coverage for general surgeries related to changing one's sex appearance: chin augmentation, laryngoplasty, liposuction, tracheal shave, facial bone reduction, rhinoplasty, facelift, etc., all for the 'dysphoric employee'.

Amazon, with its new health acquisitions, clearly has an investment in identity medicine, and if our constitutional right to free speech is the cost, so be it.

#21

Let's have no more talk of dysphoria[21]

The media is selling disembodiment as expression, for-profit, and they are including free shipping.

In less than a decade, the 'transgender human rights movement', replete with their own NGOs, has morphed from 'born in the wrong body' to 'gender identity disorder', to 'gender dysphoria', to 'gender incongruence', to 'gender identity', to 'gender expression', complete with lines of make-up, fashion and body scars.

Should it be a surprise that there is now a contagion among young women wanting to have their healthy breasts amputated? Is it possible that they are absorbing the messages that promote body

---

21 First published 28 March 2021, updated 15 October 2022. <https://www.the11thhourblog.com/post/let-s-have-no-more-talk-of-dysphoria>

dysphoria as progressive, cool, and edgy by media conglomerates selling this exact message?

The culture was primed for this contagion by the media, which we're groomed to believe, in most western cultures, is a free and open source of information in democratic societies. Remember all those stories, seven years back, of poor children "born in the wrong body," boys with a love of the color pink and hair ribbons meant to rip at our heartstrings? Stories of families with young children who like the stereotypical things of the opposite sex flooded the media, across western cultures, with the same narrative: discovery of an unacceptable identity, initial anxiety within the child and the family, and then all of them eventually overcoming the disruption. The families realized it was another 'normal' way to be human. Everyone lived happily ever after. The media coincidently forgot to mention all the medical risks and problems for the rest of the child's life.

Seven years later, we have an epidemic of young women and many young boys as well, threatening their parents with suicide if they do not agree to allow their children to take wrong sex hormones and have surgeries on their sex organs on demand. At the same time, medical professionals affirm children's disordered thinking. Advertising is nothing if not insidious which is what makes it so effective.

On one front, we have Johnson & Johnson marketing these procedures as totally routine 'cosmetic' surgeries, surgeons smiling into cameras at gender clinics, cheerleading the most macabre re-engineering of healthy human sex organs, reality TV shows and mainstream magazines celebrating the castration of young men.

Men are walking fashion runways in pregnancy prostheses, and young women are being displayed in underwear ad campaigns; their surgery scars from the amputation of healthy breasts being promoted as empowerment. Meanwhile, journalists, academics, and those engaged in politics and policy, are all being censored for attempting to critique this by the same media. Is this supposed to be an organic development across countries and media platforms simultaneously?

Hollywood stars 'parade their children' who like to wear the clothing associated with the opposite sex as little accessories in their fashionable lives for the media. Others are feeding cult-Koolaid to young people from magazine spreads with children who want these surgeries too.

While the media inundates us with these messages, taxpayers are forced to fund operations through new health insurance policies for surgeries on young people's bodies that are neither sick nor injured. All the while, gender ideology activists and their NGOs supporting the construct of 'synthetic sex medical expressions' are depathologizing this monstrosity and attempting to sell the public the idea that sex exists on a spectrum, that human sexual dimorphism is a construct, and that expressing how you feel about yourself by having your sex organs surgically rearranged is progressive. Access to wrong sex hormones is being offered to students on university campuses without medical oversight or recommendation. At the same time, LGBT organizations that fund the media in exchange for the press supporting gender industry delusions, scream, "human rights!!"

Media platforms are owned by massive corporate conglomerates that interface with the medical industrial complex (MIC). People think they are reading *Glamour*, *Vogue*, *Vanity Fair*, *Wired*, and *The New Yorker* when they are reading Conde Nast, a corporate conglomerate with a massive investment in the MIC and gender as a medical identity. Ditto for *Cosmopolitan*, *Esquire*, *Bazaar*, *Good Housekeeping*, *Oprah*, *Seventeen*, *Women's Health*, etc., which are part of the Hearst media conglomerate, with vast investments in the MIC and the gender industry. Ditto for those watching ABC, ESPN, and Touchstone Pictures (among hundreds of other media platforms) owned by Disney, yet another conglomerate with significant investments in the MIC, including the gender industry. Disney holds high prestige with the LGBT Human Rights Commission for their 'diversity and inclusion' policies which are corporate-speak for homogeneity of thought, and have funded $100 million to children's hospitals across the country, including Texas Children's Hospital and Children's Hospital of Los Angeles, both of which have gender clinics. Pity the children caught in this corporate profiteering matrix! Meredith Corporation owns *People* magazine (which covered the celebration of a young man's castration party), *Parents*, *In Style*, *Health*, *Shape*, and until about two minutes ago, owned *TIME* magazine (let's not forget their famous cover of Laverne Cox). Meredith, like any other media conglomerate, has its health platforms and investments in the MIC. *TIME* magazine (of recent Elliot Page fame) was purchased by billionaire Marc Benioff in 2018 for $57 billion. But don't expect things to get any better for an allowable critique of the gender medical industry at Benioff's new platform purchase because you'll be out of luck fast. Benioff is all on board with the violation of privacy, safety, and rights of women and girls and is jumping in where Disney left off, bestowing a whopping $100 million to another California children's hospital. And oh, look, they just happen to have a youth gender clinic too!

There aren't many media conglomerates feeding us real information, only what fits within the allowable purview of their corporate interests. They are all on board the gender-as-medical-identity train, leading us to believe this uniformity of thought is organic acceptance by the populace which encourages groupthink acquiescence. In other words, people are being brainwashed into believing that disembodiment for profiteering is a human right and that most people agree with this – when most people don't know much about what is happening because all they see are slick advertisements by the MIC-controlled media and messages from the LGBT NGO front which tell the media what to say. The mainstream media is being controlled and trained by LGBT NGOs fronting for the MIC and functioning as the arbiters of nothing less than reality itself.

We must understand that this apparatus of the gender industry is being strategically driven by capital, technological developments, and the MIC through all our institutions, corporations, and governments. While we are all arguing about what identity means as it is overlaid with sex-role stereotypes, the elites are running away with human sex. They are violating the boundary between male and female, opening markets in which our essential humanity becomes a-sky-is the-limit market to be mined.

#22

The legal construction
of the transgender child[22]

*Freedom for children and young people lies in dismantling the
culturally ascribed power of the biological.*

—*Gendered Intelligence*
(an international gender lobby group)

The 'transgender child' is a corporate, legal, and technological
construct. Its manifestation was necessary for substantiating
the evolution of an adult male fetish into an industry of owning
women's reproductive capacities via medical technology. An adult
male fetish of owning womanhood, and cutting it up for the market,
is a very hard sell for the public.

Children distressed about feeling wrong in their sexed realities,
promoted as having special human identities, needing protection
and rights, and medical manipulation, hits the marketing sweet
spot, because it cultivates our empathy.

Shortly after the two most significant and powerful LGBT
NGOs in the world emerged on the American landscape and
added the 'T' to the LGB acronym, a small, six-year-old boy, whose
name was changed to Jazz Jennings, became Hollywood's first
'transgender child'. He hit the talk show circuit, first with Barbara
Walters in 2007, and then elsewhere. That same year, his family
started a non-profit organization to normalize a medical identity,
whereby children uncomfortable with their sexed reality have their
reproductive organs medically manipulated. In the USA, Jazz has
become a household name. He has had myriad medical assaults
on his genitalia for identity purposes. A storybook for children

---

22   First published 22 October 2023. <https://www.the11thhourblog.com/post/the-
legal-construction-of-the-transgender-child>

about his life was published in 2014 by Penguin Books. That same year a male actress, Laverne Cox, posed on the cover of Mark Benioff's *TIME* magazine, announcing a "transgender tipping point." In 2015, a reality TV show documenting the assaults on Jazz's reproductive sex was aired on national television, concurring with former Olympian Bruce Jenner's debut on the cover of *Vanity Fair* magazine, claiming womanhood for himself. In 2016, Jazz was medically castrated for mass entertainment, and in 2017, he had his own Barbie doll.

Attempting to disown one's sexed reality is not a human right or a lifestyle choice. It has evolved from an orchestrated technological and corporate cultivation of dissociation from reality. It is indoctrination, being spread over technology, and through our institutions, that we can lift ourselves from the sexed roots of our humanity into another type of human.

Dentons and Thomas Reuters' Nextlaw Referral, the largest legal network in the world, have created a guide, entitled *Only Adults? Good Practices in Legal Gender Recognition for Youth.* The guide, created for the International Lesbian And Gay Youth Organization (ILGYO) provides an overview of practices for legal gender [sex] recognition for people under 18 based on self-determination. In other words, massively influential corporate structures are being used to create systemic social change to normalize, for children, that their wholly sexed reality is a set of interchangeable parts.

Let's follow the money trail back from ILGYO, the small LGBT youth non-governmental organization, for which Dentons and Reuters collaborated on the guide. ILGYO is partnered with both Transgender Europe (TGEU) and ILGA Europe, constituting an extensive funding, legal, and political apparatus driving the normalization of dissociation from sexed reality in Europe. TGEU consists of 200 member organizations across Europe and Central Asia in 50 different countries.

ILGA Europe's credo is, "bodily integrity is the principle that all people, including children, have the right to autonomy and self-determination when it comes to their own bodies." Working with the Council of Europe Committee on Bioethics, they help develop international human rights for the body integrity of those claiming synthetic – or alternate – sex identities, either for themselves or as they are imposed on children.

TGEU and ILGA are both funded to the tune of hundreds of thousands of dollars by the Arcus Foundation (AF), one of the two most potent LGBT non-governmental organizations in America. Jon Stryker, the founder of AF supports his foundation through the profits of his medical supply corporation (recently investing in the facial feminization surgery market). Stryker Medical Corporation, to which Jon Stryker is heir, is worth $133.55 billion (updated amount, April 2024), with annual revenues for 2023 projected at $19.4 billion (up from $13.6 billion in 2018).

The Dentons and Thomas Reuters Nextlaw report was designed to assist activists in several countries to bring about changes in the law allowing children to change their gender (read: sex) legally, without adult approval and without needing the approval of any authorities.

Thomas Reuters Foundation is funded by the Gill Foundation, the second most significant LGBT NGO in the world. The founder of the Gill Foundation is Tim Gill, another philanthropic billionaire who is also a friend of Jon Stryker. Gill sold his company, Quark Press, to create his foundation and has since been helping support the legal structure for manifesting the 'transgender child'. The Arcus and Gill foundations support myriad global programs to drive the idea that children can be of the opposite sex, such as Gender Spectrum, The Transgender Law Center, LAMBDA, and GLSEN (whose founder, Kevin Jennings, was brought to Arcus in 2012 as Executive Director). Another benefactor of Stryker's money is the American Civil Liberties Union (ACLU) who have created their own legal guide for 'transgender children', and their families.

This pattern of funding from the two most significant LGBT NGOs, whose founders have funneled half a billion dollars each from their personal wealth into their foundations to drive gender ideology globally, is repeated by other corporatists with heavy investments in Big Pharma. Among the many funders is George Soros. Soros, who dumped his stocks in CVS, owned $2.1 million shares in 2007, the year Jazz Jennings arrived on the talk show circuit. He has owned a significant amount of shares in Johnson & Johnson pharmaceutical giant which promotes the removal of children's reproductive organs as progressive. He is currently invested in health platforms and Salesforce Cloud Computing, whose co-founder is deeply invested in creating synthetic sex identities for children. In 2015, the year *I Am Jazz* was broadcast, Open Society Foundations created a legal guide for the 'transgender child', entitled *Trans Children and Youth*.

A guide from the Human Rights Campaign (HRC), titled *Supporting and Caring for Transgender Children* was published the year Jazz Jennings was castrated on national television.

Soros' Open Society Foundations is working to construct, along with the Gill Foundation, the Arcus Foundation, HRC, the ACLU, and gender identity organizations in Europe, the idea that children being medicalized for life is just another way to be human. This new way to be human, for children being funneled into hundreds of youth 'gender clinics', involves dangerous drugs and medical procedures that assist them in hiding the fact they are either biologically male or female. In 2013, the Arcus Foundation brought over Adrian Coman from Soros' Open Society as the Director of their Human Rights Department.

The transgender child was created to sell the deconstruction of human reproductive sex to the public. In 2012, Transgender Legal and Defense Education Fund (TLDEF), founded in 2003, filed a complaint with the Colorado Civil Rights Division on behalf of six-year-old boy, Coy, alleging that the school had violated his rights. Coy sought to use the bathrooms corresponding to his imagined identity, rather than his biological sex. His rights to violate the privacy and safety of females was upheld and seen as win for the entire state of Colorado. Colorado has been subject to the financial threat of Tim Gill and Jon Stryker's sister, Pat Stryker, for those who don't toe the line on new LGBT policy dictates that support the 'T'.

TLDEF is funded by the Arcus Foundation and the Gill Foundation and is a national partner of the pharma giant, Gilead. Gilead Sciences recently committed $4.5 million in grants to transgender support and advocacy groups – $2.5 million more than the company had originally planned. Gilead opened the doors to grant seekers in September 2023 with the promise of $2 million total in funding to groups that help 'transgender people'. Gilead is also funding doctors who promote the highly contentious, off-label use of puberty blockers for children.

Corporations and legal entities worldwide are using the strategy of tying children's body dysphoria, a once very rare medical condition, to an adult male fetish. This male fetish of being a woman is becoming viable for the men who seek this validation, through advancements in medical reproductive technology and the creation of synthetic sex.

Of the most prominent law firms in the world (ranked by revenue), most have accepted and invested in 'T' as it is attached to LGB. New corporate protections have been established, and diversity, inclusion, and equity departments have been added. Pride platforms, ally seminars, and educational initiatives for gender identity have all been woven into the international legal frameworks of these law firms.

Societies are not being rapidly overhauled for people's identities, children's body dysphoria, or some amorphous 'gender identity'. They are being overhauled to change the way we think of ourselves as a species: a sexually dimorphic species. Children are being groomed to think of themselves as parts, not wholly sexed beings. If we wish to stop this assault on children, we must be clear on where it comes from, where it is going and why it is happening, or children will continue to be used as eugenic fodder for a future in which they will be reduced to commodities.

#23

The World Economic Forum and Holtzbrinck Publishing Group: How their transhumanist-gender-identity propaganda is disseminated[23]

The World Economic Forum (WEF) is becoming a de facto government, supported by its members: some of the richest and most influential people in the world. Larry Fink of BlackRock, the world's preeminent asset management firm with $10 trillion in assets, is a partner of WEF, was a recent speaker there, and sits on their board of trustees. It is hardly a secret at this point that part of the plans for society and human beings, outlined by WEF, is the biological and digital augmentation of our species, which will take us beyond our current evolution. Part of this forced evolution will include genetic engineering, DNA manipulation and reproducing our species via technology, sans coitus.

---

23 First published 10 June 2023. <https://jbilek.substack.com/p/the-world-economic-forum-and-holtzbrinck>

The marketing of this forced evolution of our species is everywhere, the propaganda relentless, but not just through corporate advertising and in mainstream media, controlled by their conglomerate heads, and ultimately by their financiers.

Holtzbrinck Group Publishing (HGP) conglomerate is another partner of the World Economic Forum, and one of the top five global publishing conglomerates in the world which has its own 'queer' department. Biotechnologies, that allow people who pose as the opposite sex via technology and drugs, to conceive children after being sterilized by a medical assault on their sex, are being reported on by BMC Publishing, part of Springer Nature Publishing (SNP). Both of these publishing houses are part of the Holtzbrinck Group Publishing (HGP) conglomerate.

SNP has recently been called out by academics and biologists for prioritizing transactivist politics over science.

HGP and BMC created a joint venture in 2015 by merging Macmillan Science and Education with Springer + Business Media. A man who desires to own womanhood is the Corporate Risk and Insurance Manager at HGP. HGP scientific platforms like BMC and Springer Nature publish unsupported disingenuous 'scientific' information about gender identity with articles that deny sex. The owner of HGP, Dr Stefan von Holtzbrinck, is also a founder and sits on the board of the Max Planck Foundation (MPF), one of the largest and most prestigious science-funding foundations in Germany. In 2018, MPQueer, from the Max Planck Society PhD Student network, was formed to counter any resistance to 'queers' within the organization. Holtzbrinck has an annual 'diversity day' at the publishing group, a diversity specialist, and an LGBTQIA+ network – 'Queer@Holtzbrinck'.

Macmillan, a subsidiary of Holtzbrinck, has its own queer collection, with titles such as *I'm Not A Girl*, *This Body I Wore*, and *Transgender China*. Holtzbrinck also published *The Genesis Machine*, a non-fiction book speculating that synthetic biology promises, according to its authors, to

... reveal how life is created and how it can be re-created, enabling scientists to rewrite the rules of our reality. It could help us, for example, heal without prescription medications, grow meat without harvesting animals, or confront our looming climate catastrophe. Synthetic biology will determine the ways in which we conceive future generations and how we define family.

It's not just Holtzbrinck Publishing Conglomerate and WEF pushing a transhumanist agenda via gender identity and the queering of humanity.

Author Susan Stryker's book, *Transgender History*, was published by Seal Press, an imprint of Hachette Book Group (HBG). Hachette Book Group (HBG) is a publishing company owned by Hachette Livre, the largest publishing company in France, and the third largest trade and educational publisher in the world. Along with Holtzbrinck, it is one of the top five publishing houses globally. Hachette Book Group is amplifying its queer collection for Pride month, with titles such as *Gender Magic*, and *Baby Making for Everyone*.

Susan Stryker is a queer academic and transsexual. He is the author of *Transgender History* (2008), a book about the technological future of reproduction. In it he quotes *Unzipped Genes* (1997), another book about the technological future of reproduction, authored by the author of the first 'gender bill', Martine Rothblatt. In the quote, Stryker waxes poetic about Frankenstein's monster. He compares Mary Shelley's monster's travails to his own, having a technologically constructed synthetic sex.

"My Words to Victor Frankenstein Above the Village of Chamounix, written in 1974" are the following:

> I have asked the Miltonic questions Shelley poses in the epigraph of Frankenstein: 'Did I request thee, Maker, from my clay to mould me man? Did I solicit thee from darkness to promote me?' With one voice, her monster and I answer 'no' without debasing ourselves, for we have done the hard work of constituting ourselves on our own terms, against the natural

order. Though we forego the privilege of naturalness, we are not deterred, for we ally ourselves with the chaos and blackness from which Nature spills forth.

What is a queer academic? 'Queer' used to mean different. It was pejorative, but then was reclaimed by LGBTI activists, as in "we're here, we're queer, get used to it." It developed as an intellectual academic theory to challenge the notion of a static sexual identity and advanced to reframe homosexuality and bisexuality on par with heterosexuality, not subordinate to it, as sexual orientations. It could not quite reach that paradigm because heterosexuality is the way our species reproduces.

Enter: technology. Suddenly this paradigm seems possible, as sexual dimorphism is being deconstructed, via the gender industry, in the name of a civil rights movement for people who are same-sex attracted. The deconstruction of sexual dimorphism is being framed as liberation to support technological developments in sexual reproduction and synthetic biology which are poised to remove sexual reproduction from the bedroom to the laboratory, finally putting people's same-sex attraction on par with heterosexuality in a future of irrelevancy.

Can men have babies? Can women have penises? Should categories of sex be obliterated socially? Sex is being socially queered everywhere we turn to make way for technological and biotech developments which are positioned to usurp women's reproductive capacities. The surrogacy and fertility markets are growing rapidly. There is research into womb implants for men, and men can be loosely equipped through technology to lactate and chest-feed children. Women who have the lion's share of responsibility for gestating new life are being linguistically and legally erased, their sports and safe houses, designated by sex, opened to men. Men are claiming womanhood for themselves, and children are being groomed for industrial body dissociation to indoctrinate them away from natural reproduction and groomed to have their sexual boundaries violated. Most people don't realize this is a transhumanist religious ideology that ultimately forgoes the body for a technological supremacy of the mind.

The Partnership for Global LGBTI Equality (PGLE) is a coalition of organizations purportedly committed to leveraging their individual and collective advocacy to accelerate LGBTI equality and inclusion in the workplace and in the broader communities in which they operate. The Partnership is supported by the Office of the United Nations High Commissioner for Human Rights and is operated in collaboration with the WEF. This partnership is part of how gender ideology, or transhumanism, is being rapidly driven into various countries across the world. It supports the advancements in technologies that will 'queer' sex and change us fundamentally as a species. It is the reason we hear so much about 'gender identity', and 'transgenderism' which are not the fads many think they are.

Societies organized around our species' sexual dimorphism are being rapidly overhauled to erase it, to have it eventually usurped by tech.

Legislation is being passed toward what is being called "fertility equality" for LGBTI people. We see gay men creating international conferences on technological reproduction and surrogacy. Others are speaking about the dissolution of sexual orientation that will meld into a cacophony of sexual appetites that are separate from our reproductive sex organs. Fetishes, which are dissociative, objectifying and compulsive are being promoted everywhere as positive, from Pride parades to corporate board rooms.

Children are being taught in their schools that to dissociate from their sexed reality is just another way to be human. They are being inundated with graphic sexual material on their social media and in their libraries to prepare them for a future of technological reproduction, a severing of biological ties to families of origin, their own bodies and coitus from intimacy.

Make no mistake, it is not same-sex attraction that brought us to this point. It is the *corporatization* of sexual orientation, the creation of identities based on sexual attraction, and the need for corporate entities to open markets or wither in the capitalist marketplace. There is no way to open markets in sexual identity with a sexually dimorphic species. The boundary of male and female must be broken to create more market opportunities from our sexed realities, and potentialities for future pursuits in augmenting humanity via technological reproduction. The WEF in partnering with two of the top publishing conglomerates – Holtzbrinck and Hachette – is helping to drive the propaganda that we are not a sexually dimorphic species. This will see our sex boundaries obliterated, if we do not resist soon.

#24

Genspect: The new LGBT NGO framework[24]

Every good cause begins as a movement, becomes a business and eventually degenerates into a racket.

—Eric Hoffer

Genspect, an organization originating to help children process their feelings about what is marketed to them as gender identity, and parents who've lost their children because of it, has morphed into a new type of LGBT NGO. Its messaging, like the word 'transgender' itself, is without borders and people are noticing. On November 4–5 2023, Genspect had a major conference in Denver, Colorado with speakers discussing everything having to do with the gender ideology leviathan. The Bigger Picture conference certainly was big.

I write about the money that drives gender ideology propaganda, which makes it look like a medical issue (and simultaneously akin to the human rights issues for lesbian, gay, and bisexual individuals), so I don't invest in the idea that children are having a medical problem. Therefore, I no longer support Genspect. Of course, once you start treating a propaganda problem medically, you create a medical problem on top of a propaganda problem, which then feeds the narrative that it's a medical problem. Just look at poor Jazz Jennings, a young boy who once liked sparkles and rainbows, who is now a grown man posing as a woman, and who's been through medical castration on his once healthy body, and two subsequent surgeries on his synthetic genitalia.

Since I have researched this issue for a decade, followers of my work have asked me to weigh in on the confusion and anger some felt at seeing a man parading his autogynephilic fetish and

---

24 First published 12 November 2023. <https://jbilek.substack.com/p/genspect-the-new-lgbt-ngo-framework>

marketing his book about his paraphilia at the recent Genspect conference. His book promotes the destigmatization of his fetish by rebranding his autogynephilic compulsion 'autoheterosexuality'.

Autogynephilia, otherwise known as transsexualism, is the male sexual compulsion to own womanhood. It is at the root of what is becoming an industry in synthetic sex characteristic commodities, being marketed to children.

Genspect exists to help the families harmed by the normalization and industrialization of this fetish-turned-predatory-industry, and the fetishists themselves. Attempting to help them both, as a public organization, was a bad idea to begin with, and now that Genspect is growing, so are their problems.

I had a look at Genspect's conference schedule. I've come to respect the work of several of the speakers who were showcasing their analysis. But putting them all together in one conference belied the lack of focus this organization has that generates so much conflict. The itinerary mirrored the hydra of gender ideology itself, and this hydra is staggeringly incoherent when you look at the entire beast at once.

Genspect wants to be too many things to too many people. It wants to serve two masters, just like LGBT NGOs who want to support LGB and TQ+. Everything after the LGB in the acronym attempts to undermine the sexual dimorphism upon which LGBs exist (along with the rest of us).

Genspect wants to hold onto a medical (psychiatric) idea of gender, while trying to undo the harms the medical profession is doing to kids in creating imaginary sex categories. But unless medical professionals are moving children and families away from a medical paradigm and helping them to understand how they have been indoctrinated, they simply magnify the problem.

There are no 'transgender children' (or adults for that matter), and there are certainly no children with the adult male sexual fetish of autogynephilia, which the medical industry is marketing.

Dr Miriam Grossman is the one therapist I know who uses her skills as a psychiatrist to help people caught in this cult to process their feelings, while speaking out publicly and clearly that *children are suffering highly advanced and penetrating, technological and political, cult indoctrination.*

Dr Grossman is also in private practice. She has not attempted to turn herself into an NGO.

Genspect creates a medical feedback loop because it has created an NGO. It doesn't try to help move people out of the problem by offering support and then education about what has happened to them (indoctrination). They support its continuation, like all LGBT NGOs are doing (I wrote about this in 2022).

Just like transsexualism has been rebranded to 'transgenderism' by other LGBT NGOs, to make transsexualism more appealing for marketing to the masses, Genspect has rebranded the LGBT NGO model to a Gender Framework, making it more welcoming and novel for people who don't know what is going on. The idea is to capture them to follow a more moderate way of dealing with the problem. (Not too quick with the drugs and scalpels, please!) But it is selling the same narrative. It promotes 'gender' and 'transgenderism' as real as if they have coherent definitions. It tells families that medical (psychiatric) attention can help people. It promotes individuals who attempt to disown their sexed reality as spokespeople, and they suggest that children have a multiplicity of 'genders'. This has been going on since Genspect started. Its new 'Gender Frame' is of course the same gender spectrum that other LGBT NGOs suggest exists, with less of a thrust on medicalization. This is expressed clearly on its website:

> Our international organization includes professionals, 'trans
> people', detransitioners, and parent groups who work together
> to advocate for a non-medicalized approach to gender diversity.

Is an entire organization of medical and other professionals needed to explain to children that they can wear clothes typically associated with the opposite sex? What is meant by 'gender diversity'?

Genspect also claims to support LGB people, and that it is intolerant of homophobia, while supporting the concept of 'transgender people', and a spectrum of genders ('diversity of genders'), which has helped undermine the entire progress made by the LGB civil rights movement since its inception. A diversity of gender promotes the violation of the boundary between the sexes. This supports the duplicitousness of the LGBT model, like other LGBT NGOs do.

Genspect has no interest in tearing down the gender industry. It is now an international organization that relies on the continuance and growth of there being a gender problem if it is to subsist, just like any LGBT NGO.

This isn't advanced physics. It is a standard operating procedure. If I have shown nothing else in my work, I have shown how this works. Just look at Genspect's position:

> There are many routes that may lead to the development of distress over an individual's gender. Equally, there are just as many routes out of such distress. That's why we would like to see a wider range of treatment options and more evidence-based approaches to gender-questioning children and young people.

More 'treatments'! More research! More funding for the many different reasons children might be distressed about 'their gender', sans propaganda that there is such a thing.

Marketing is key, and Genspect's marketing is getting tighter and slicker, if not more coherent. Its euphemisms for what amount to a eugenics project are no less disturbing than any other LGBT NGO. 'Gender questioning children' and expressing 'distress about their gender' do nothing to convey the brutality underway in this industry.

This could go on indefinitely. And rest assured it will, until we decide to stop it. I'm not holding my breath; I just think it's a good use of my time to try and beat back this dangerous, repetitive, nonsense. For those thinking I am too extreme, someone needs to be the adult in the room. I don't think Genspect is fully conscious of what it is supporting or how it is turning into the new LGBT NGO model. The people in Genspect are not malevolent, but neither are most people functioning inside most LGBT NGOs today, saying that they want to protect 'gender children'. They become excited about helping. They get other people involved. They grow their NGO to get information out to more people. They lack self-awareness because a lot of people are now involved. They've secured some wins. Expressed concerns, outside of their narrative, are seen as a threat and shut down. The women expressing safeguarding concerns about an adult male fetishist at the Genspect conference were framed by supporters of Genspect as ego-driven purists, narcissists, pearl clutching feminists. Extreme, not unlike the TRA mantras – Nazi, far right, bigots – meant to shut them up.

The more transsexualism is standardized and discussed by Genspect and other LGBT NGOs, the more men present themselves with it. They want to be talked about, noticed, and examined, and more damage is incurred by them doing so. With this reinforcing feedback loop, more men with this compulsion are being put in positions of political power, like the recent state senate win by Danica Roem in Virginia who clearly stated that he will go about changing policy for 'trans children'. Does he mean children with an adult male fetish like his own (should we be allowing men to project their fetishes onto children?), children who have a type of body dysphoria, children who have autism or who are presenting with confusion about their sexed reality for other reasons, children who are indoctrinated on social media by influencers and medical professionals, or kids who are expressing a rebellion about strict sex role stereotypes? What exactly does he mean by 'transgender children'?

Genspect seems to be setting up this same projection of the adult male fetish of autogynephilia onto children, creating a whole new prototype of kids (teens with AGP) and the experts to 'treat' them. Again, I don't take obliviousness as malicious intent, but in the end, does it matter?

Genspect doesn't threaten the status quo. If it did, it would not have been allowed to grow as it has.

People who address the problem with straightforward political campaigns that don't medicalize the issue of male fetishists create far less confusion for people and are viciously attacked. Kellie-Jay Keen, a women's rights campaigner in the UK, was almost trampled to death in New Zealand in 2023 for promoting the fact that women are adult human females.

Genspect, just like every other LGBT NGO, thinks it is solving a problem when it *is* the problem. It is solidifying gender ideology. After a decade of resistance, we are desperate for saviors and are grasping at straws. But you cannot win a political battle engineered to undermine humanity's sexed reality, which is marketed to us as a medical issue, with a counter medical paradigm.

#25
Autogynephilic confessions and the sacrifice of women's humanity[25]

In the age of 24/7 tech surveillance and confession capitalism, whereby ordinary individuals confess the most intimate details of their lives, and offer thoughts for money, attention, or likes on social media, privacy is in very short supply. Each day, life in general looks more and more like an episode of the Jerry Springer show, as noted by journalist Julian Vigo, except we can't go home when the show is over. The show doesn't end.

The normalization of men's sexual fetishes played out in society is eroding our privacy further. In the past couple of years, there has been a spate of men who either used to identify as female or still do,

25 First published 10 February 2021, updated 16 October 2022. <https://www.
the11thhourblog.com/post/autogynephilic-confessions-and-the-sacrifice-of-
women-s-humanity>

who now perform public confessions about their autogynephilia. These confessions lull us into complacency about what this fetish does in the material world, keeping us wrapped up in the pornified, dissociated, and objectifying psyche of men, where we are used to living. The erosion of privacy for others who do not consent to be privy to others' fetishistic displays is not the only thing being cultivated. The intensified dehumanization of females laid on the sacrificial altar of men's sexual gratification is also being demanded. The dehumanization of females is okay, as long as it alleviates men's 'dysphoria'.

How awful it must be to have a daughter today and to know that she will walk through the world where her biology, her humanity, can be reduced to synthetic parts for men's sexual gratification and that this is normal. Her sexual objectification will no longer be seen as sexual objectification. It will have been erased, along with her humanity, having become any man's identity who chooses it.

James Shupe, in an article in *Intellectual Takeout* in 2020, takes us on a journey from his self-ID as female, then as a non-binary person, to the accolades of many, including the media, and back to an embrace of his actual biological reality and his autogynephilic fetish. During this journey, which feels a lot like the story of the boy who cried wolf, Shupe gives us the intimate details of his 'sins' (BDSM, sex clubs, etc.). He wants us to believe he is making amends and starting a new life, but his sexual proclivities are still shoved in our faces. Women who've had their sex brutalized by the medical industrial complex and who have grown into an understanding of what has happened to them, sound, comparatively, like the stories of those returning from a war zone, compelling us to understand their feeble attempts to find a way out of sexual objectification, subordination, and homophobia.

In June of 2020, Corinna Cohn made his true confession via an article in *Quillette*, which is far more palatable but centers his 'affliction', his feelings and his suffering with no mention of the harm in parading his paraphilia in public, as he is coming to terms with being an autogynephile. He feels "displaced as a transsexual" because dissociation and sexual objectification of others have become cool and trendy. Poor Corinna. Try being an object. There is zero acknowledgment of the continued harm or suffering caused to females when we are publicly reduced to parts one can buy in a Sears catalog or surgeon's office to get off on. We are dehumanized, even as Cohn seeks to understand what feminists think. He takes the advice of one that he should not be ashamed to be transsexual. Perhaps his fantasy should not be shamed. Maybe it is only the public parading of his fetish that reduces women to parts and violates everyone's privacy not to be engaged in other people's sexual proclivities that should be shamed.

Kate Madden made his true confession in November 2020 in a tell-all video about his autogynephilia, to cultivate sympathy for his 'condition'. I want to know where the sympathy resides for the women exposed to a grown man impersonating them for his sexual gratification.

Our sexual objectification and dehumanization are the cost of alleviating these men's 'dysphoria'. In what universe should one person's objectification be used to mitigate another's discomfort while evoking public sympathy?

Inspireverse is a YouTube platform giving voice to yet another male with this 'disorder' of objectifying female biology for his sexual gratification, who thinks breaking it down for the public so they can understand it, should cultivate our sympathies and make society a better place to live. For whom, I might ask?

Certainly not for women who are treated like objects in this scenario. "It's not easy for these men to come forward to share their need to objectify women's biology sexually," says this YouTuber. We not only get to hear the grisly details of this person's sexual disorder and listen to him ask for our sympathy, but he adds the sexual objectification of animals as well. To his mind, this is 'brain mapping' gone awry for some people, himself included. Women as human beings escape him completely.

Never once is the normalization of the sexual objectification of women mentioned by any of these men. They are oblivious in the extreme. Never is porn mentioned in the equation, or the capitalist system taking the bullet train of advanced technologies that drive this normalization of females as objects across the globe like the black plague on steroids. They want their paraphilia normalized and understood in society so they don't have to hide it.

The promotion of this paraphilia by corporate culture, and now in these 'poor me' confessionals of adult men, is not an accident. Whether all men pretending to be women have the fetish of autogynephilia is irrelevant, it is at the root of the gender industry. The fetish of objectifying female biology is driving the normalization of body dissociation. It is intensifying the objectification of females globally as we are erased in language and law to appease this paraphilia and the men who have it. Other women have honed in on this. Sheila Jeffreys, Sue Donym, Dr Em, and Janice Raymond come immediately to mind. This recent spate of true confessions is all part of this normalization process.

Taking your eyes off the gender industry leviathan of body dissociation for profit for one minute, and the technology driving it, is one minute more that you will spend in a fog. The gender industry is a multi-headed serpent, a corporate monster opening markets via the promotion of women as parts to acquire. It must be slain, lest females are laid to waste. What is at stake is our social privacy, sexual privacy, cohesion, our roots as humans in sexual dimorphism, and our tether to reality. Ask yourself one last question. Are you willing to pay the price?

#26

Activists and the artificially manufactured sexes of the gender industry[26]

Many activists today are attempting to push back against a medical-tech industry that is assaulting children's reproductive organs, and the human sex binary itself. This industry not only poses serious risks to children and adults, and societal norms, but also promotes an ideology suggesting that individuals can simply choose their biological sex.

These activists are engaged in a battle against what I term the 'gender industry', a construct largely driven by adult male fantasies of appropriating womanhood as they intersect with the medical-tech industry. This industry not only undermines the rights of children and women based on biological sex but also attempts

---

26 First published 18 February 2024. <https://jbilek.substack.com/p/activists-and-the-artificially-manufactured>

to establish a narrative that recognizes a third category of sexed human beings outside the binary of male and female, requiring special rights and considerations.

By employing opposite-sex pronouns and amplifying the voices of individuals with artificially constructed sex characteristics, some of these activists are inadvertently contributing to the legitimization of this corporately fabricated category of humanity. Others have built organizations in an effort to offer emotional help to families with a loved one taking on an alternative sex identity but have wound up supporting the initial problem: a corporate and technological construct of an alternative type of human being.

The legal advancements made in the name of protecting this manufactured third sex category of humanity rely on linguistic manipulations that distort the very foundation of human existence. For activists adopting such language, attempting to curry inroads of communication with people who have been captured by the ideology, any success they acquire will only provide temporary relief, as it fails to address the underlying issue: the proliferation of technologically manipulated humans who make up the alternative sex category and where it is leading.

The notion of a third type of human, divorced from biological reality, serves as a pretext for the sale of artificial sex characteristics, and ultimately paves the way for a technological revolution in human reproduction. This process moves us away from our intimate connections to biology, each other, and will, if successful, make women obsolete.

The gender industry thrives on dismantling the understanding of biological sexes and promotes an untold number of fluid sexual identities and orientations. As the demand for products supporting technologically engineered humans grows, fueled by the allure of 'technology as a life-giving god', societal norms are rapidly evolving, accompanied by legislative changes to accommodate these new identities. However, it's crucial to recognize that these identities are artificially constructed through a combination of drugs, surgeries, language manipulation, and technology. They are devoid of any inherent reality.

Most activists attempting to resist the gender industry have only scratched the surface of the technological underpinnings of the market in deconstructing sex, narrowly focusing on the recent medical scandals, oversexualization of children and intrusions into women's rights, without fully grasping the broader implications at play.

Tying this construct of another kind of human to an already established human rights apparatus for people with same-sex attraction, via the LGB NGO and political infrastructure, was strategic genius. This has cultivated public sympathy for a third type of human that simply does not exist. It is purely a corporate, technological fabrication, at least so far.

The SoftBank Group's pursuit of a $100 billion AI chip venture, code-named Izanagi that will rival Nvidia, inspired by the Japanese god of creation, epitomizes the use of technology toward creating a post-biological existence for humanity, and imagining a tech god that will do the creating. SoftBank is renowned for its LGBTQ initiatives and 'inclusive' work environment, and has received the highest Gold rating in the PRIDE Index.

Silicon Valley has been reporting on the melding of man and machine since early 2000s, and predicted humans will be partnering with robots in technology marriages in the future. This is a trajectory toward a technological usurpation of creation itself.

The oversexualization of children on their tech platforms and in schools, and especially on their social media, are sexually traumatizing them into a state of dissociation from their bodies, while they become further entrenched in technology, and are groomed in schools to believe that their parents do not always have their best interests at heart. This is occurring while women, the natural life-givers, are being erased in language and law, and reduced to inhuman caricatures in public displays of male fetishes.

Figures like Martine Rothblatt, a transsexual transhumanist invested in the furtherance of transsexual identities into a transhumanist realm, the future of technological reproduction, gene editing, AI, and human surveillance, and his mentor of Google fame, Ray Kurzweil, envision a future where technology transcends human limitations, blurring the lines between biology and machinery. Kurzweil, a Google advisor, envisions a future where humanity, augmented by technology, transcends age-old limitations, potentially altering the nature of mortality. He consistently insists on the emergence of god-like tech and a future humanity that is post-biological, not gestated by women, but by technology. Rothblatt, along with building a tech-centered religion, has outlined principles resembling a blueprint for the modern gender movement, seeking to overcome what he terms 'fleshism'. Kurzweil's employer, Google, the pioneering corporation in the transhumanist domain, is assisting the Trevor Project, an LGBT NGO, in developing an AI platform for children, and furthering the narrative for children that they can choose their sex.

When we shift the lens on the third sex category of humanity presented to us, from human rights to business and technological developments, it becomes evident that the gender industry is primarily profit driven, with an eye toward controlling human evolution. Activists leveraging individuals with artificially constructed sex characteristics, to sway those misled by, and invested in, the human rights frame, reinforce the legitimacy of this harmful construct. Historically, this approach has proven to be counterproductive since the industry's infancy in the 1960s. It is now a much stronger business model.

Efforts to combat the cultural ramifications of the gender industry must not turn away from confronting its technological dimension and its promotion of a technologically fabricated third type of human. Legal victories against this corporate illusion are likely to be short-lived, as the industry continues to thrive with substantial legal and financial backing, unless we can claw back the right to speak intelligibly, so everyone can understand what is at stake.

The top one hundred highest-earning international law firms worldwide all have LGBT+ platforms supporting the gender industry. This support champions the destruction of healthy human reproductive organs, the use of drugs and surgeries that radically compromise health, and linguistic fabrications that confuse people who have already been captivated by a nefarious narrative. Many have been led to the belief of a transcendent third category of human beings, and the ideas that people can change sex and that reproductive sex exists on a spectrum. These law firms offer pro bono legal assistance, allyship programs, health insurance, guidebooks for legal strategies that support a third category of human, and even organize Pride parades for individuals seeking to override their biological sex through technology and drugs.

The widespread support of major corporations and financial firms for profitable medical-tech interventions promoted by the gender industry, further underscores the profit-driven nature of this enterprise and its roots in human engineering. Despite efforts to portray technologically and medically constructed sex characteristics as unique identities, they remain myths perpetuated for profit. There are only males and females of our species.

Activists must focus on addressing *the root causes* perpetuating the profit-driven interests of the gender industry while safeguarding the rights of individuals and protecting children. Challenging its false narratives and advocating for truth in language that supports our biological reality against a synthetic one, will be essential in effecting lasting change.

#27

The industry of artificial sex characteristics and the dissolution of our human boundaries[27]

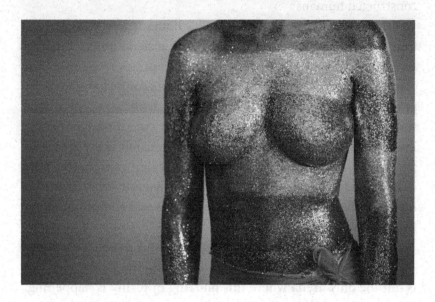

The artificial sex characteristics of the gender industry are not real. They are products in a developing medical-tech market. They do not inherently alter the individuals who acquire them or endow them with any special human attributes. Instead, they primarily influence our perception of reality, serving the profit-driven agenda of the industry.

Although still in its infancy, this industry focused on self-actualized sex through commodification is experiencing rapid growth. It is imperative that we grasp the nature of this situation

---

27 First published 27 February 2024. <https://jbilek.substack.com/p/the-industry-of-artificial-sex-characteristics> <https://www.the11thhourblog.com/post/the-industry-of-artificial-sex-characteristics-and-the-dissolution-of-our-human-boundaries>

to avoid being drawn into the constructed virtual reality it seeks to impose upon us. We must question whether we want to inhabit a manufactured environment where individuals are reduced to commodities and reproduction is facilitated through medical technology, or as part of the natural world. How far is too far in experimenting with the line between reality and technologically constructed humans?

Many individuals hesitate to speak honestly about the gender industry, fearing misunderstanding or accusations of bigotry. But it's important to recognize bigotry applies to people, not commercial products. Presently, there exists confusion where the products of the synthetic sex market – the artificially constructed sex characteristics of the gender industry – are mistaken for the individuals who purchase them. This confusion is escalating as people try to navigate a marketing campaign of human rights designated for commodities. We are in dangerous territory when humanity is being reduced to commodities and commodities are being given human rights.

Humanity is being blurred intentionally for a virtual construct – beings beyond our currently sexed borders. The gender industry is not the only arena where this blurring of reality is happening, but sex is foundational to our existence as a species, which makes it crucial for people to understand what is transpiring. We must get beyond our fear of talking about this industry in real terms, instead of the language the market has set with its advertising slogans. 'Trans rights are human rights' is a slogan that infers the commodities of artificial sex characteristics are people. They are not.

This confusion is not an accident. It is a deliberate strategy of the ad for synthetic sex. Artificial sex characteristics, crafted through medical technology, are being promoted under the guise of human rights advocacy precisely because it blurs the lines between the products of the gender industry and the people who purchase the products. This branding aims to convey a sense of uniqueness and transformation to consumers.

All marketing works in this way. The ad campaign signals to the world the place of the consumer of the product in society, and cultivates the perceptions of others through advertising. A woman driving a Mercedes-Benz is bound to get a very different welcome at valet parking than the woman driving a Ford. The brand of car doesn't change anything fundamental about her. It creates an illusion that she is a more worthy individual because she can afford a Mercedes-Benz in a society that values wealth over human integrity.

The artificial sex characteristics of the medical-tech industry are no different.

The gender industry operates by deconstructing reproductive sex and commodifying its components, including eggs, sperm, wombs, synthetic hormones, breasts, penises, and vaginas. Children are increasingly exposed to gender ideology in their schools and other learning environments, and on their social media where they spend many more hours than previous generations. They are encouraged to view themselves as commodities rather than wholly, sexed beings. This indoctrination, coupled with exposure to explicit sexual material, contributes to the dissociation from their innate biological reality.

Efforts to challenge the destructiveness of the gender industry often become mired in debates about fairness, surrounding identities pertaining to sex and societal roles, detracting from the underlying economic motivations.

Institutions, governments, and corporations invest in this industry for its profitability, viewing individuals not as complete human beings but as marketable parts. Notions of privacy become eroded within this paradigm. Commodities don't need privacy. People do.

It's essential to dispel the notion of 'gender people' and recognize individuals as consumers caught up in a market driven by financial interests. The industry's proliferation signifies a broader societal deconstruction, reducing individuals to mere commodities devoid of inherent worth or boundaries. The ethical ramifications of this dehumanization cannot be understated. The dissolution of social cohesion is already creating chaos and the harm being meted out to children is unconscionable.

Many groups and organizations now forming in attempts to resist the harms of the gender industry are using consumers of artificial sex characteristics as symbols of solidarity or understanding. They fail to acknowledge the diverse motivations behind these consumer choices. Individuals who opt for synthetic sex characteristics remain male or female, and any perceived transformation is a product of marketing rather than inherent change. By using consumers of artificial sex characteristics as props, they bolster the industry and the illusion that these consumers are a type of person. I am not a new type of person if I purchase a Mercedes-Benz. The same is true of people who consume synthetic sex characteristics. They are consumers of a product.

The synthetic sex industry is medical dehumanization. It is unethical in all its forms. The fact this must be argued, or that people have come to be afraid to offend anyone by saying so, tells us exactly how far the dehumanization of all of us has already progressed.

In confronting the gender industry, it's imperative to dispel the illusion of a battle for human rights against a fabricated construct. Instead, we must recognize it as a manifestation of medical-technological commodification and work towards restoring the dignity, boundaries, and integrity of individuals within society.

Conclusion

If I have learned anything in the past decade of researching the gender industry as a front for a transhumanist paradigm, I know that resisting it demands no compromise. We must tell the absolute truth about what it is and what it is doing.

The corporate agenda to deconstruct human sex is a Goliath of power playing on our empathy, dividing us by positioning us against their construct of alternative humans who need special protections. The laws transhumanists are passing, and their attempts to rapidly overhaul our societies, institutions, and language, are all formulated to advance a transformation of humanity and the reality that we live in. They are not hiding this. It is up to each of us to open our eyes and understand this transformation. If we refuse to speak about it, in fear that others won't understand us, or that we might lose our jobs, our families, or our friends, or that our organizations will be cut out of the fight, then we should just give up now. The blogs in this book are only the tip of the spear.

Every action against the gender industry is vital, but the most important aspect of resistance is to let go of the illusion that there is another type of human outside the borders of our sexed species, or that there is a coherent group of individuals that warrants the kind of attack on humanity, society, and reality, like the one we are witnessing. We have been pummeled for a decade with high-tech propaganda claiming that a suffering group needs us. It is an illusion.

It is terrifying to contemplate what losing this battle will mean, and it is just as frightening to contemplate acting against the gender industry as it becomes increasingly more totalitarian. It seems insurmountable and, the truth be told, it may be. But freedom is worth fighting for. Fighting against a technocratic assault on children's reproductive organs and their minds, so that they may have a future as part of the natural world, is worth everything. Silence is no longer acceptable.

List of acronyms

ACLU	American Civil Liberties Union
ADHD	attention deficit hyperactivity disorder
ADI	Advancing Dignity Initiative
AF	Arcus Foundation
AI	artificial intelligence
APF	American Psychological Foundation
ARC	Allied Rainbow Communities International
AWS	Amazon Web Services
BLM	Black Lives Matter
BSR	Businesses for Social Responsibility
CSE	Committee on Schools and Education
CoCM	Collaborative Care Model
ESG	Environmental, Social and Corporate Governance
EY	Ernst & Young
D&I	Diversity and Inclusion
DEI	Diversity, Equity and Inclusion
FINAARGIT	International Feminist Network Against All Artificial Reproduction, Gender Ideology and Transhumanism
FoSE	Future of Sex Education Initiative
GATE	Global Action for Trans Equality
GD	Gender Dissent
GeMS	Gender Multispeciality Service at Boston Children's Hospital
GI	gender identity
GI	Gendered Intelligence
GLSEN	Gay, Lesbian and Straight Education Network
GPP	Global Philanthropy Project

HBG	Hachette Book Group
HGP	Holtzbrinck Group Publishing
HIPAA	The Health Insurance Portability and Accountability Act
HRC	The American Human Rights Campaign
IBGR	International Bill of Gender Rights
ICD-11	International Classification of Diseases (11th revision)
ICTLEP	International Conference on Transgender Law and Employment Policy
ILGA	International Lesbian, Gay, Bisexual, Trans and Intersex Association
ILGYO	International Lesbian and Gay Youth Organization
ITF	International Trans Fund
IVG	in-vitro gametogenesis
LGBTIQ+	lesbian gay bisexual transgender intersex queer and others
LF	Left Forum
MAP	LGBT Movement Advancement Project
MIC	Medical Industrial Complex
MPF	Max Planck Foundation
NASA	National Aeronautics and Space Administration
NFL	National Football League
NGO	non government organization
NIIMBL	National Institute for Innovation in Manufacturing Biopharmaceuticals
NSES	National Sex Education Standards
OWS	Occupy Wall Street
PGA	Parliamentarians for Global Action
PGLE	Partnership for Global LGBTI Equality
POW	Prisoners of War
PPFA	Planned Parenthood Federation of America
PRI	Principles for Responsible Investing

QTRL	Queer, Trans Research Lab
SDG	Sustainable Development Goals
SI	Salk Institute
SIECUS	Sexuality Information and Education Council of the United States
SOGI	Sexual Orientation Gender Identity
SNP	Springer Nature Publishing
SSIs	synthetic sex identities
TENI	Transgender Equality Network Ireland
TGEU	Transgender Europe
TLDEF	Transgender Legal and Defense Education Fund
TMC	techno-medical complex
UCLA	University of California
UCSD	University of California San Diego
UN	United Nations
UNESCO	United Nations Educational, Scientific and Cultural Organization
US	United States
WEF	World Economic Forum
WISE	Working to Institutionalize Sex Education
WLU	Wilfrid Laurier University
WPATH	World Professional Association of Transgender Health
YP	Yogyakarta Principles

Acknowledgments

To each one of you holding the line for reality, it is your resolve in love and courage that keeps me firmly planted. Thank you for speaking up, for resisting, for telling the truth when it has been in short supply. Thank you for taking the risk. Thank you for sharing my work. There are so many of you, that I'd need another book just to name you all. Some of you I have never even met, but I've been moved by your efforts and your support.

Some must be named as crucial to my sanity in all this, and still others in the practical work of getting things done. To Joey Brite, Brandon Showalter, Davina Allen, Stella Morabito, Kara Dansky, Rachel Berry, Natalie Ballard, and Nancy Robertson, my sincerest gratitude.

For those who have contributed to *The 11th Hour* blog, you have my deepest appreciation.

Last, but not least, if not for the love of my family and friends, I could not stay grounded. It is our laughter, and our joy, that fortifies me in this fight. Thank you.

Index

Also published by Spinifex Press

Laura Lecuona
Gender Identity: Lies and Dangers

The concept of *gender* is central to a vaguely progressive-looking set of ideas based on the maxim that people possess a so-called 'gender identity'. This book is essential reading for the urgently needed conversation we need to have about whose interests are being served with the advancement of transgender ideology and what this means for women's sex-based rights.

ISBN 9781925950908   ebook available

Kajsa Ekis Ekman
On the Meaning of Sex:
Thoughts about the New Definition of Woman

Translated by Kristina Mäki

In this groundbreaking book, Swedish feminist and Marxist, Kajsa Ekis Ekman, traces the ideological roots of the new definition of woman. She shows how biological determinism is back – but minus the biology. Instead, there are stereotypes: womanhood is no longer about having a vagina, but pink ribbons and dolls. Masculinity is no longer synonymous with having a penis but with war and machines.

ISBN 9781925950663   ebook available

Cherry Smiley
Not Sacred, Not Squaws: Indigenous Feminism Redefined

Smiley analyses colonization and proposes a decolonized feminism enlivened by Indigenous feminist theory. Building on the work of grassroots radical feminist theorists, Cherry Smiley outlines a female-centered theory of colonization and describes the historical and contemporary landscape in which male violence against Indigenous women in Canada and New Zealand is the norm.

ISBN 9781925950564   ebook available

Janice Raymond
Doublethink: A Feminist Challenge to Transgenderism

In an age when falsehoods are commonly taken as truth, Janice Raymond's new book illuminates the 'doublethink' of a transgender movement that is able to define men as women, women as men, he as she, dissent as heresy, science as sham, and critics as fascists.

ISBN 9781925950380   ebook available

Sheila Jeffreys
Penile Imperialism:
The Male Sex Right and Women's Subordination

In this blisteringly persuasive and piercingly intelligent book, Sheila Jeffreys argues that women live under penile imperialism, a regime in which men are assumed to have a 'sex right' of access to the bodies of women and girls.

ISBN 9781925950700   ebook available

Susan Hawthorne
Vortex: The Crisis of Patriarchy

In this enlightening yet devastating book, Susan Hawthorne writes with clarity and incisiveness on how patriarchy is wreaking destruction on the planet and on communities. The twin mantras of globalisation and growth expounded by the neoliberalism that has hijacked the planet are revealed in all their shabby deception.

ISBN 9781925950168   ebook available

Heather Brunskell-Evans
Transgender Body Politics

Heather Brunskell-Evans shows how a regressive men's rights movement is posing a massive threat to the human rights of women and children everywhere. In a chilling twist, when feminists critique the patriarchal status quo it is now they who are alleged to be extremists for not allowing men's interests to control the political narrative. Institutions whose purpose is to defend human rights now interpret truth speech as hate speech, and endorse the no-platforming of women as ethical.

ISBN 9781925950229   ebook available

Silvia Guerini
From the 'Neutral' Body to the Posthuman Cyborg:
A Critique of Gender Ideology

This book is a radical critique of gender ideology and transhuman design. Silvia Guerini shows how the TQ+ rights agenda is being pushed by eugenicist capitalist technocrats at the top Big Business, Big Philanthropy, Big Tech and Big Pharma. She argues that dissociation from our gendered bodies leads to dissociation with reality and the erasure of women.

ISBN 9781925950885   ebook available

Max Robinson
Detransition: Beyond Before and After

Detransition is a far-reaching discussion of women's struggles to survive under patriarchy, which draws upon a legacy of radical and lesbian feminist ideas to arrive at conclusions. Robinson's bold discussion of both transition and detransition is meant to provoke a much-needed conversation about who benefits from transgender medicine and who has to bear the hidden cost of these interventions.

ISBN 9781925950403   ebook available

If you would like to know more about
Spinifex Press, write to us for a free catalogue, visit our
website or email us for further information
on how to subscribe to our monthly newsletter.

Spinifex Press
PO Box 105
Mission Beach QLD 4852
Australia

www.spinifexpress.com.au
women@spinifexpress.com.au